A FALCON GUIDE®

Exploring Series

Explore!
Shasta Country

A Guide to Exploring the Great Outdoors

Bruce Grubbs

FALCONGUIDE®

GUILFORD, CONNECTICUT
HELENA, MONTANA

AN IMPRINT OF THE GLOBE PEQUOT PRESS

A FALCON GUIDE®

Maps by Bruce Grubbs © Morris Book Publishing, LLC
All photos by the author

ISSN: 1932-3506
ISBN-13: 978-0-7627-3412-2
ISBN-10: 0-7627-3412-4

Manufactured in the United States of America
First Edition/First Printing

Contents

Overview

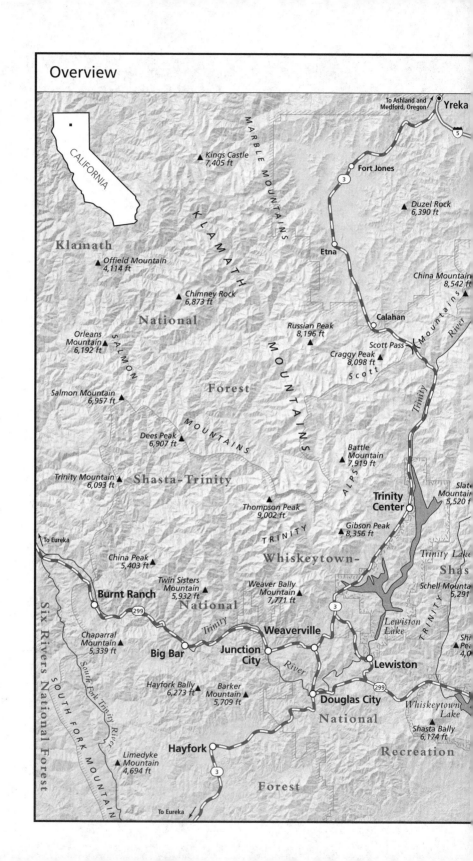

CALIFORNIA

To Ashland and Medford, Oregon
Yreka
5

Kings Castle
7,405 ft

Fort Jones
3

Duzel Rock
6,390 ft

MARBLE MOUNTAINS

Klamath

Etna

China Mountain
8,542 ft

Offield Mountain
4,114 ft

KLAMATH

Chimney Rock
6,873 ft

National

Russian Peak
8,196 ft

Calahan

Orleans
Mountain
6,192 ft

SALMON

Scott Pass

Craggy Peak
8,098 ft

Mountains

River

Scott

Forest

Salmon Mountain
6,957 ft

MOUNTAINS

Trinity

Dees Peak
6,907 ft

Battle
Mountain
7,919 ft

ALPS

Trinity Mountain
6,093 ft

Shasta-Trinity

Thompson Peak
9,002 ft

Trinity
Center

Slate
Mountain
5,520 ft

Gibson Peak
8,356 ft

To Eureka

TRINITY

Whiskeytown-

Trinity Lake

Shas

China Peak
5,403 ft

Twin Sisters
Mountain
5,932 ft

Weaver Bally
Mountain
7,771 ft

3

Schell Mountain
5,291

Burnt Ranch
299

National

TRINITY

Lewiston
Lake

Chaparral
Mountain
5,339 ft

Trinity

Weaverville

Shi
Pea
4,0

Big Bar

Junction
City

River

Lewiston

Six Rivers National Forest

Hayfork Bally
6,273 ft

Barker
Mountain
5,709 ft

299

Douglas City

Whiskeytown
Lake

SOUTH FORK

South Fork Trinity River

National

Limedyke
Mountain
4,694 ft

Hayfork

3

Shasta Bally
6,174 ft

Recreation

MOUNTAIN

Forest

To Eureka

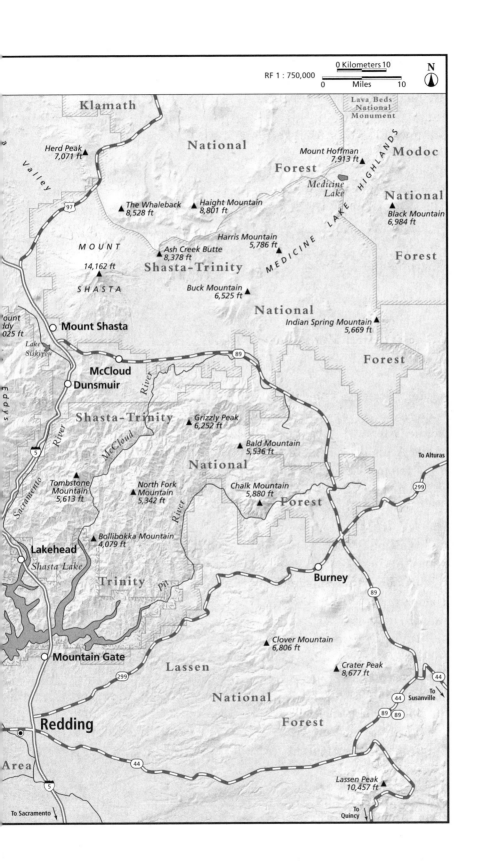

0 Kilometers 10

0 Miles 10

N

Klamath

Lava Beds
National
Monument

Herd Peak
7,071 ft

National

Mount Hoffman
7,913 ft

Modoc

Forest

Valley

97

The Whaleback
8,528 ft

Haight Mountain
8,801 ft

Medicine
Lake

National

Black Mountain
6,984 ft

MEDICINE LAKE HIGHLANDS

MOUNT

14,162 ft

SHASTA

Ash Creek Butte
8,378 ft

Shasta-Trinity

Harris Mountain
5,786 ft

Forest

Buck Mountain
6,525 ft

National

Indian Spring Mountain
5,669 ft

ount
ldy
025 ft

Mount Shasta

Lake
Siskiyou

McCloud

Dunsmuir

River

89

Forest

Shasta-Trinity

McCloud River

River

Grizzly Peak
6,252 ft

Bald Mountain
5,536 ft

To Alturas

National

Chalk Mountain
5,880 ft

Forest

299

5

Sacramento River

Tombstone
Mountain
5,613 ft

North Fork
Mountain
5,342 ft

Bollibokka Mountain
4,079 ft

Lakehead

Shasta Lake

Trinity

Pit

Burney

89

Mountain Gate

299

Lassen

Clover Mountain
6,806 ft

Crater Peak
8,677 ft

44

To
Susanville

National

44

89 89

Redding

Forest

44

Area

5

Lassen Peak
10,457 ft

To Sacramento

To
Quincy

Map Legend

Boundaries

~~	National/Wilderness Boundary
/////////	National Forest/Recreation Area Boundary

Transportation

═══70═══	Interstate
═40══9══	U.S., State Highway
—————	Primary Roads
——709——	Other Roads
══709══	Unpaved Road
= = = = =	Unimproved Road
▬ ▬ ▬ ▬ ▬	Featured Unimproved Road
▬ ▬ ▬ ▬	Featured Trail
▪▪▪▪▪▪▪▪▪▪▪	Optional Featured Trail
- - - - - - -	Other Trail
——▬——	Tunnel
┼┼┼┼┼┼┼	Railroad

Hydrology

∿	River/Creek
～ ⌃ ⌃	Intermittent Stream
℅	Spring
∥	Falls
⬤⬤	Lake

Physiography

×	Spot Elevation
)(	Pass
▲	Peak

Symbols

🚶	Trailhead
🅿	Parking
♿	Restroom
❷	Information
🏠	Ranger Station
⚓	River Access
⛵	Boat Launch
⚓	Marina
⚲	Beach
⌂	Campground
▲	Primitive/Backcountry Camp
⬧	Cabin/Lodge
†	Cemetery
⊞	Picnic Area
○	Town
◉	Viewpoint
▪	Point of Interest
✗	Mine
•—•	Gate
⨝	Bridge
⚠	Caution

Acknowledgments

I'd like to thank everyone who made this book possible, including all the fine people at The Globe Pequot Press, and especially my editors, Bill Schneider and Lynn Zelem. Thanks also to Stephen Stringall, map coordinator at The Globe Pequot Press, for patiently working with me to produce the maps. I'd also like to thank the personnel of the Shasta–Trinity National Forest, Whiskeytown–Shasta–Trinity National Recreation Area, the Bureau of Land Management, and Castle Crags State Park for their assistance. And finally, warm thanks to Duart Martin for supporting and encouraging this project at every step.

Introduction

This guide covers an area of northern California loosely termed the Shasta region, a mountainous piece of country encompassing the southern end of the Cascade Mountains and a large chunk of the Klamath Mountains. The towering volcanic cone of Mount Shasta, the second highest of the Cascade volcanoes at 14,162 feet, dominates the region and is visible for hundreds of miles. Mount Shasta towers thousands of feet above timberline, and the upper portion of the mountain is draped with permanent snowfields and glaciers. The lower, heavily forested mountain ranges south and west of Mount Shasta are the Klamath Mountains, which are further subdivided into several ranges. These include the Salmon Mountains, Trinity Alps, Trinity Mountains, Scott Mountains, and Castle Crags, among others. Numerous summits in the Trinity Alps reach above timberline, and the area is dotted with alpine lakes and meadows. This complex terrain is drained primarily by the Shasta and Trinity Rivers and their tributaries. Four major reservoirs, Shasta, Whiskeytown, Trinity, and Lewiston Lakes, are the centerpieces of the lower elevation country. (Trinity Lake is shown as Claire Engle Lake on some maps. To avoid confusion, the name Trinity Lake is used throughout this book.) The lowest elevations in the Shasta region are found at Shasta Lake. This huge reservoir tops out at 1,066 feet when full.

As you would expect with all this variety, there are many fine recreational opportunities in the Shasta region. These include fishing and boating on the lakes and rivers, hiking, riding, and mountain biking the trails, climbing the peaks and rock faces, sightseeing along the roads, camping in the forest, and exploring the geology and natural history. A section of the Pacific Crest National Scenic Trail traverses the region on its route from Mexico to Canada.

The purpose of *Explore! Shasta Country* is to introduce you to this varied region and provide an overview of the many recreational activities. The emphasis is on self-propelled, low-impact activities.

How to Use This Guide

Using the Trail Descriptions

Mileages

Trail mileages are for the total distance of a hike or ride. If the hike or ride is out-and-back, that is, you return the same way you came, the total distance given includes the return trip. For one-way trails, which require a car shuttle, the total distance assumes you will actually leave a shuttle vehicle at the end of the trail and do it one way. Of course, if you do a one-way trail as an out-and-back, you'll travel twice as far as the total distance given. Loop trail total distance is for the loop section that you trek one way as well as any cherrystem sections that are traveled both out and back. Mileages were carefully measured with topographic mapping software. This was done for consistency, so that while the book's mileages may not always agree with official distances or trail signs, you can confidently compare trail mileages within the book.

Difficulty Ratings

All hikes and rides are rated as easy, moderate, or difficult, a highly subjective rating that nevertheless should help you decide which trails are for you. Generally, easy trails are fairly short, can be done in an hour or two, and have little elevation change, so nearly anyone should be able to do these trails. A few of the trails are wheelchair-accessible; this fact is noted in the Special Considerations section. Moderate trails are longer and often have significant elevation change, so you should be in reasonable shape for riding or hiking and have a good bike or good footwear and a pack to carry water and other essentials. Difficult trails are long and always have large elevation changes. Although none of the routes in this book are cross-country, remember that trail conditions can change because of storms, wildfires, or just plain lack of use and maintenance. Before starting your trek, check with the nearest ranger station for the latest information on trail conditions.

Route Finding

Don't depend on trail signs for finding your way: Signs are often missing and sometimes inaccurate. While most of the trails described in this book were chosen because they are well used and easy to follow, there are many official trails shown on maps that are faint and receive little maintenance, as well as informal trails created by other hikers who may or may not know where they are going. Cairned routes, marked by piles of rock, should be followed with a healthy skepticism. Cairns are often constructed casually, with no thought to the overall route, and even by lost people.

Be responsible for your own route finding, and don't leave it to others. Use a good map (see the next section), and keep track of your location as you go. You may even want to note your position and the time on the map occasionally. In any case, if you track your position faithfully, you'll never be puzzled when you reach a trail junction with a confusing or missing sign. Tracking your location on a map will also help you judge your rate of progress, so you know when to turn back or when you'll arrive at a spring or planned campsite.

Mount Shasta.

Also, decide on a baseline before venturing into the backcountry. A baseline is an unmistakable linear feature that forms a boundary along one side of your hiking area that you can hike to and be certain you won't miss. Major roads or trails are the best baselines. For example, if you were planning a hike into the east end of the Trinity Alps, a good baseline would be Highway 3, which runs along the east base of the mountains. In the event you became completely lost in this area, you would be assured of reaching the highway by hiking generally east. A compass is the best means of determining direction, but you can also use the sun or stars. Of course, walking to your baseline would probably be a long walk that would take you far from the trailhead where you left your car, so it is always a last resort if you get completely lost and can't find the trail or retrace your steps.

Always carry a high-quality compass—which is not the same as an expensive compass. Silva, Brunton, and others make basic, high-quality, liquid-filled compasses that cost very little. Although you won't often need your compass, when you do need it, you'll need it badly—in thick forest under a cloudy sky, for example.

Maps

The maps in this book that depict a detailed close-up of an area use elevation tints, called hypsometry, to portray relief. Each gray tone represents a range of equal elevation, as shown in the scale key with the map. These maps will give you a good idea of elevation gain and loss. The darker tones are lower elevations and the lighter grays are higher elevations. The lighter the tone, the higher the elevation. Narrow bands of different gray tones spaced closely together indicate steep terrain, whereas wider bands indicate areas of more gradual slope.

Maps that show larger geographic areas use shaded, or shadow, relief. Shadow relief does not represent elevation; it demonstrates slope or relative steepness. This gives an almost 3-D perspective of the physiography of a region and will help you see where ranges and valleys are.

As mentioned earlier, all of the hikes and rides in this book are on trails. A good overview map for the area covered by this book is the Shasta–Trinity National Forest map, available from the U.S. Forest Service. This map shows highways, national forest roads, and trails, as well as ranger stations, visitor centers, picnic areas, campgrounds, boat launch sites, marinas, and other facilities.

Mountain bikers, hikers, and boaters in the Whiskeytown–Shasta–Trinity National Recreation Area will find the topographic map of the same name published by Earthwalk Press to be very useful.

Wilderness hikers, climbers, and backcountry skiers will find the U.S. Forest Service wilderness maps *Trinity Alps Wilderness* and *Mount Shasta and Castle Crags Wildernesses* especially useful. These are topographic maps with detailed trail and terrain information.

All these maps are available from U.S. Forest Service and National Park Service ranger stations and visitor centers in the Shasta area, and also from outdoor shops.

Those who wish to expand their exploration of the Shasta region to the less-used trails and to cross-country travel and peak bagging find the 7.5-minute series of topographic maps published by the U.S. Geological Survey to be useful or even necessary. These are derived from aerial photos and are extremely accurate when it comes to terrain and natural features, but because the topos, as they are also known, are not revised very often, trail, road, and other man-made features are usually out of date. Nevertheless, the 7.5-minute topo's fine depiction of topography is indispensable for the off-trail hiker, especially when used in conjunction with the two U.S. Forest Service wilderness maps.

The 7.5-minute topographic maps are available directly from the U.S. Geological Survey, and from some visitor centers and ranger stations, as well as from outdoor shops. You can also buy digitized sets of topographic maps for use on a computer from several companies. The software that comes with these map sets lets you measure trail distances, make detailed trip plans, up- and download Global Positioning System coordinates to a GPS receiver, annotate maps with personal information, and print custom maps for specific areas.

Share the Trail

Most of the wilderness trails in this book are open to horseback riders as well as hikers, and many of the trails outside the wilderness areas are open to mountain bikers as well. Horses always have the right of way over hikers and cyclists, both of which should move off the trail downhill and remain still until the horses have passed. Talking quietly to the riders helps convince the horses that you are a person and not some weird monster with a hump on its back. Don't make sudden movements or noises.

Technically, hikers have the right of way over cyclists, but in practice it's more reasonable for hikers to step off the trail so as to avoid forcing the riders off trail. On their part, cyclists should be courteous, always ride under control, and warn hikers of their approach.

Zero Impact

Being just a few hours drive from major population centers, the Shasta region is heavily used. The backcountry can handle a lot more people if they work to minimize their impact. Most backcountry users probably don't intentionally abuse the land, thinking that cutting switchbacks on trails, dropping orange peels, building campfires, trying to burn their trash, picking flowers, and disturbing artifacts don't matter. But they do. Multiply each little impact by thousands of visitors, and soon the wild places look beaten down and hammered. Each visitor owes it to the thousands that will follow to have as close to zero impact as possible.

Three Falcon Principles of Zero Impact

- Leave with everything you brought in.
- Leave no sign of your visit.
- Leave the landscape as you found it.

Most of us know better than to litter, but how many people think of orange peels as litter? Even such organic litter takes a long time to degrade. Tiny pieces

Boulder Lake, Trinity Alps.

of foil or paper from food wrappers may not seem like much, but they last for dozens of years and soon give the ground that littered, overused look. Likewise with cigarette butts. Consider picking up other people's litter on your way out. It adds little to your load, and a great deal of self-satisfaction.

Stay on the trail. Cutting switchbacks actually costs more energy than it saves and leads to erosion and loss of vegetation. Most trail work is done by volunteers since land management agencies just don't have the budget these days to pay for trail maintenance. By cutting switchbacks, you're just creating more work for a fellow cyclist or hiker who's given up some of his or her riding or hiking time to keep the trails in good shape.

Don't ever pick flowers or disturb artifacts, historical objects, or any natural features. The next visitors want to see these things, too. Federal and state law protects both historic and prehistoric artifacts. Report any such disturbance to the nearest ranger station or visitor center.

Avoid making loud noises on the trail or camp. You may be having a good time, but don't ruin other people's backcountry experience. If you have a dog with you, don't allow it to bark, especially in camp.

Dogs are allowed in most of the Shasta area, but they must be under control at all times. If your dog runs up to other people and doesn't respond to verbal commands, it is not under control and must be kept on a leash. Along roads and in campgrounds and picnic areas of the Whiskeytown Unit of the Whiskeytown–Shasta–Trinity National Recreation Area, dogs must be on a leash no longer than 6 feet. Remember that every unpleasant dog–human encounter increases the number of places closed to dogs.

When nature calls, use public restrooms at visitor centers, campgrounds, or trailheads whenever possible. If these facilities are present, it means that human use of the area is too great for natural disposal systems.

In the backcountry, relieve yourself at least 200 feet from springs and creeks. To take advantage of the natural, biological disposal system present in soil, find a site in organic rather than sandy soil, if possible. Dig a cathole about 6 to 8 inches deep, staying within the organic layer of the soil. Carefully cover the hole afterward. Some hikers carry a plastic trowel for this purpose. Pack out all used toilet paper and personal hygiene items in double plastic bags. NEVER burn toilet paper: Numerous wildfires have been started this way.

Keep all camp waste, including toothpaste, dishwater, and soap, at least 200 feet from water. Never wash yourself or dishes in a spring or stream. Water sources are all too easily contaminated. Remember that many other people will need the same water sources, and that wildlife may depend on them.

Camping is available at numerous public developed sites throughout the Shasta region. Most of these campgrounds are accessible by car, but there are some on the large lakes that are accessible only by boat. All of the camp-grounds charge a fee. You can also camp away from developed campsites throughout the Shasta–Trinity National Forest and the Whiskeytown–Shasta–Trinity National Recreation Area, with the exceptions of the Whiskeytown Unit and Castle Crags State Park, which allow camping only in the developed campgrounds. There is a fourteen-day stay limit throughout the Shasta–Trinity National Forest.

There are numerous private campgrounds throughout the Shasta region. These generally offer amenities such as showers and recreational vehicle hookups not found in the public campgrounds.

Anyone planning to build a campfire outside a developed campground must have a campfire permit, available from any U.S. Forest Service office. During periods of high fire danger, campfires may be restricted to camp-grounds only, or banned completely. Wilderness campers should strongly con-sider cooking on a lightweight backpacking stove instead of a campfire, as many popular campsites are showing the effects of excessive fire building and wood gathering.

People planning to camp overnight or longer within the Trinity Alps, Cas-tle Crags, or Mount Shasta Wilderness Areas must have a wilderness permit, which is available at ranger stations and trailheads. In addition, climbers on Mount Shasta must have a "Summit Pass" to climb above 10,000 feet. Fees are charged for these permits.

Strictly follow the pack-in/pack-out rule. Whether you are vehicle camping, boating, day hiking, rock climbing, on horseback, mountain biking, or back-packing—if you carried it in, you can and should carry it out.

Boating Regulations

The following boating regulations apply to all lakes and reservoirs in the Mount Shasta area, including Shasta, Trinity, Lewiston, and Whiskeytown Lakes. There may be additional regulations at individual lakes; refer to the appropri-ate chapter of the book for details.

Registration and Permits

All vessels must be registered and numbered except boats propelled manually and sailboats less than 8 feet in length without other means of propulsion. Out-of-state registration is good for ninety days.

General Rules

All boaters are responsible for knowing the boating regulations, boat opera-tions, and the conduct of passengers. The operator must also know the proper procedures in the event of a boating accident.

Careless or Negligent Operation

This includes riding on the bow, gunwale, or transom of a boat without a protective railing while under way; maneuvering towed skiers or devices so as to pass the towline over another vessel; and operating under the influence of alcohol or drugs. Other actions, such as speeding or skiing in confined or restricted areas, or buzzing other boats or people, may also be considered reckless operation.

Speed

All boats, including personal watercraft, are limited to 5 miles per hour (mph) within 100 feet of swimmers (except for skiers) and within 200 feet of swimming beaches, landings, docks, and boat ramps. Many coves are marked with buoys restricting speed to 5 mph. There is a nighttime 15 mph speed limit in effect from a half hour after sunset to a half hour before sunrise.

Waterskiing

Portions of the lakes are closed to waterskiing; these areas are generally marked by buoys. Waterskiing is prohibited between sunset and sunrise. In addition to the boat operator, there must be an observer at least twelve years of age to watch the person being towed.

Personal (Powered) Watercraft

A lanyard must be attached between the personal watercraft and the operator's clothing. The operator cannot jump a wake within 100 feet of a boat, and personal watercraft cannot be driven toward another boat. Personal watercraft cannot be operated from a half hour after sunset to a half hour before sunrise.

Engine Noise

Engines must be muffled or otherwise prevented from exceeding 82 decibels adjusted (dBA) at 50 feet. Boats manufactured before January 1, 1978, may run at levels up to 86 dBA. Boats with unbaffled exhaust pipes do not meet these standards.

Sanitation

Holding tanks may not be dumped in the lakes or into floating toilets, and they may only be emptied at approved marina pumping stations.

Moorage

Docking is limited to ten to fifteen minutes at U.S. Forest Service courtesy docks, and boats 26 feet or longer may not use Forest Service docks. Residential occupancy is not permitted at marinas. Some shoreline areas are closed to public use, and boats may not be moored in these areas. Boats may not be left unattended for more than twenty-four hours except at approved marinas and docks. Boaters may not camp within 200 feet of a developed recreation site.

Fire Permits

During fire season (generally May through October), fire permits are required when using portable stoves, hibachis, barbecues, or campfires on the shoreline or on board when the boat is touching the shore. Fire permits are not required for stoves built into the vessel or for campfires in developed campgrounds.

Required Equipment

All boats must have wearable flotation devices for every person on board. All boats over 16 feet must have one throwable flotation device for the boat. The flotation devices must be in serviceable condition, without broken straps, missing hardware, or missing or defaced approval numbers. Wearable devices must be in the proper sizes for the occupants and immediately available. The throwable device must be immediately accessible.

A portable fire extinguisher or fire extinguisher system must be on all motorboats with enclosed fuel tanks or engines. All motorboats except outboards must have ventilation and backfire control systems.

Horns or whistles are required on all vessels 16 feet or longer, and all vessels (including canoes and kayaks) must have some efficient sound signal other than voice.

Running lights are required on all vessels between sunset and sunrise. Manually propelled vessels such as canoes and kayaks must have at least one handheld white light.

Make It a Safe Trip

While the Shasta backcountry is as safe as any other, being prepared greatly increases your safety and that of your party.

Being prepared for a hike, rock climb, or bike ride is more than just filling your hydration bladder and blasting off. Give a little thought to what could happen. Changes in the weather, an injury such as a sprained ankle, losing the trail, or overestimating your party's abilities can turn an easy outing into a scary epic.

Know your limitations. Be realistic about your level of physical and mental fitness for a given backcountry trek. Allow plenty of time so you won't be stressed out trying to reach camp or trailhead as the sun sinks to the horizon. Be willing to turn back if the outing is taking too long or a member of the group is having difficulty.

Check the weather forecast. In the mountains, an unusually hot spell can be as dangerous as an unexpected winter snowstorm. Summer often brings afternoon thunderstorms with lightning, hail, and sudden heavy rain. Plan to be off high ridges and peaks by midday during thunderstorm weather. Winter brings storms that can last for days, bringing rain or snow to the valleys and snow and high wind to the mountains.

Avoid traveling alone unless you are fit and experienced, and always leave a detailed trip plan and your time of return with a reliable person who knows who to call if you are overdue. A trip plan is also a good idea with a group. Even if you're confident the group can handle an injury or problem, it's always comforting to know that help will come. I prefer leaving a copy of my map with the route and any planned campsites marked, as well as the location and description of my vehicle and license number.

Learn first aid and basic survival skills in advance.

Don't eat wild plants unless you know what you are doing.

Before you leave the trailhead, study the maps and learn as much as you can about the route. Plan your outing and know what time you have to turn back or be at the halfway point in order to return to the trailhead or reach a good campsite or spring before dark.

Keep track of your progress on your map, even if you're on an easy trail. That way you can never become lost. You also know whether you are making reasonable progress toward your goal.

Don't exhaust yourself or members of your party by traveling too fast. A group should move at the speed of its slowest member. Faster hikers can take advantage of the leisurely pace to look around or even explore side hikes. If anyone expresses reservations about the trail, route, ride, or climb, back off. And take plenty of rest breaks. Remember, you're out there to have fun, not to prove anything.

If you do get confused about your location, stop, sit down, have some water and munchies, and think about it. Chances are all you'll have to do is backtrack a bit to find the trail. Note your present location, then scout back along the way you came, looking for the trail or trail markers. Leave someone at the spot where you lost the trail as a reference point, and stay within sight or at least hearing of that person. If you can't find the trail by backtracking, scout around your reference point in expanding circles. Have a look at your map and see if you can determine where the trail went. Never set off blindly cross-country without the trail. The old saw about following a stream downhill to civilization is problematic in this area because many canyons are blocked and made nearly impassable by deadfall.

In the rare case of getting completely lost, or being stranded because of injury, storm, or nightfall, stay put, provide shelter for the victim and the rest of the party, and plan on sending two people for help as soon as it's safe to do so. Never leave an injured person alone, even in parties of two. Signal for help instead.

If you have a cell phone, try it, but don't count on it working. You may get a usable signal on the high ridges and peaks, but deep in the valleys and canyons you probably won't. Be familiar with the traditional methods of signaling for help. Three of anything—three shouts, blasts on a whistle, three columns of smoke or three fires, or three flashes of light—is the international distress signal. Mirror flashes are especially effective in sunny weather, when they can be seen 100 miles away. Practice with a signal mirror ahead of time, following the instructions that came with the mirror. The general technique is to sight through the sighting hole at your target, then move the mirror until there's a bright spot of sunlight on your target. This indicates that you're reflecting the sun directly at your target. Now, tap the mirror lightly to set up a flashing, twinkling appearance to the reflected sunlight so you'll catch the observer's eye. If the sun is low behind you, have someone stand in front of you with a second mirror and reflect the sun into your signal mirror. Signal mirrors are especially good for signaling aircraft.

Carry a basic first-aid, repair, and survival kit, containing at least the following: adhesive bandages, medical tape, gauze pads, a role of gauze, antiseptic ointment, moleskin, snakebite kit, sewing needle and thread, compass, whistle, signal mirror, flashlight or headlamp, lighter or other fire starter, water purification tablets, a space rescue blanket, and a small booklet of first aid and survival instructions. You should be able to treat minor injuries such as cuts or scrapes and blisters, and stabilize victims of more serious injuries, as well as repair common problems with your gear, such as failed stitches, broken buckles or straps, tears in pack fabric, and missing parts such as clevis pins.

Avoid all wild animals. Feeding animals causes them to become dependent on human food and lose their natural fear of humans, which could lead to a dangerous future encounter and result in the destruction of the animal. Any mammal can carry rabies. See the Animals Hazards section for more information.

Weather

The Shasta region lies in the southern Cascade Mountains, a long chain of mountains stretching from northern California to southern British Columbia. Named because of the range's numerous streams and waterfalls, the Cascades wring a lot of moisture out of storms coming ashore from the Pacific Ocean, and the Shasta area is no exception. Winter storms are common from October into May. These storms often bring heavy rain to the valleys, and deep snow and high wind to the mountains. The snow level often drops to the lowest valleys during midwinter. Snow can fall on the mountains in any month, though it is less likely to occur during the summer. Late May through September is generally dry, though storms can strike at any time of the year. Thunderstorms can also occur during the summer, usually presaged by small cumulus clouds that appear over the peaks by late morning. If these clouds start to build vertically, be on the lookout for thunderstorms, lightning, high wind, heavy rain, and hail, and get off exposed ridges and peaks.

Forest fire danger increases as the forest dries out during the summer, and by August and September the conditions may become extreme. In periods of high fire danger, campfires and smoking are usually prohibited.

Mount Shasta rises more than 10,000 feet above its base, and like other isolated mountains it generates its own weather. This is largely because the mountain forms an obstacle to storm winds, much like a boulder in a stream, causing the wind to accelerate over the mountain. High wind and heavy snow can occur in any month on Mount Shasta, and all climbers venturing above timberline (8,000 to 9,000 feet) must have adequate clothing, especially wind gear, and be prepared for sudden changes in the weather.

Often the first sign of an oncoming storm is the appearance of lens-shaped, or *lenticular*, clouds over the peaks. Mount Shasta is renowned for its spectacular lenticular clouds, which often stack up several layers deep over the mountain and extend for tens of miles downwind. Though the clouds themselves are stationary, they are constantly re-forming as moisture-laden air is forced over the mountain by high wind. As the air rises on the upwind side of the peak and cools, moisture condenses out to form the lenticular cloud. On the lee side of the mountain, the air descends and warms, causing the tiny cloud-forming water droplets to dissipate.

The formation of a lenticular cloud cap on or above the summit of any peak, especially on Mount Shasta, always means high wind on the upper reaches of the mountain, and is usually a sign of an approaching storm. As the storm nears and the atmosphere becomes moister, the lenticular cloud often grows thicker and descends lower on the mountain. Climbers should heed this warning and descend.

Summer often brings hot weather to the river valleys and the lower elevations at Shasta, Whiskeytown, Trinity, and Lewiston Lakes. While this is a great time to play in or on the water, remember that rivers and lakes can still be very cold.

Heat and Dehydration

Summer heat is a serious hazard at the lower elevations in the Shasta area. During hot weather, it is safer as well as more enjoyable to hike early in the day, or at higher elevations, to avoid the afternoon heat. Always take plenty of water, even when the weather isn't scorching hot. People active in hot weather often need a gallon or more of water per day. Sport drinks that replace electrolytes are also useful. Protection both from the heat and the sun is important: A lightweight sun hat is essential, as are good sunglasses that protect your eyes from damaging infrared and ultraviolet radiation.

Prolonged dehydration and exposure to heat can lead to heat exhaustion, in which the body's heat-regulating mechanism begins to break down. Symptoms include weakness, pale, clammy skin, profuse sweating, and possibly unconsciousness. Move the victim to as cool a place as possible, provide shade and electrolyte replacement drinks, and help the body's cooling efforts by removing excess clothing and providing ventilation.

If untreated, heat exposure can result in sunstroke, a life-threatening medical emergency in which the body's heat regulation system stops working entirely. Sunstroke comes on suddenly and is marked by hot, dry skin as opposed to the pale, clammy skin of heat exhaustion victims. Additional symptoms include a full, fast pulse, rapid breathing that later becomes shallow and faint, dilated pupils, early loss of consciousness, involuntary muscle twitching, convulsions, and body temperature of 105 degrees Fahrenheit and higher. Treat the victim immediately by moving him or her to a cool location, removing as much clothing as possible, making certain the airway is open, and using wet cloths or water to reduce body temperature. If cold packs are available, they should be placed around the neck, under the arms, and at the ankles, where blood vessels lie close to the skin. Transport the victim to medical care as soon as possible.

Hypothermia

Even in the summer, mountain nights can be downright cold. Temperature drops of 50 degrees Fahrenheit are possible during afternoon thundershowers. Windy, rainy winter storms are especially dangerous. Continuous exposure to chilling weather, when your body is steadily losing more heat than it produces, can slowly lower your body temperature, resulting in hypothermia.

Hypothermia is a life-threatening condition. Its initial symptoms are subtle and can easily be missed by the inexperienced, but that is the stage at which field treatment is the most effective. Episodes of shivering are the first sign that the body is losing heat—the shivering mechanism increases production of heat by muscle action. Although breathing and pulse usually remain normal during this stage, grogginess and muddled thinking are often present, which makes it difficult to recognize hypothermia in yourself. If a member of the party seems confused about where he or she is or the goal for the outing, be on the alert.

As hypothermia becomes worse, shivering becomes violent. This is the first sign that the body is losing control of its heat-producing mechanism. A marked inability to think and a short attention span, along with slow, shallow breathing and a slow, weak pulse, are serious warning signs. At this stage, you have a medical emergency, and the victim must be rewarmed with external heat, as his or her body is no longer capable of producing enough heat to warm itself. The best source of heat is other people. Ideally, someone should share a sleeping bag with the victim. Hot water bottles wrapped in clothing can be used, but care must be taken not to burn the victim, who can't sense that objects against his or her skin are too hot. Hot drinks can help, but only if the victim is fully conscious.

Severe hypothermia is present when shivering stops, followed by unconsciousness, little or no breathing, and a weak, irregular, or nonexistent pulse. The victim's only hope of survival is immediate transport to a medical facility.

Clearly, prevention is the best treatment for hypothermia. It can be completely prevented by wearing enough warm and protective clothing to avoid chilling, and by eating and drinking regularly so that your body continues to produce heat. During the winter or in the high country, be prepared for weather changes with several layers of clothing, including wicking underwear, synthetic pants and shirts, a pile or fleece jacket, and a wind and waterproof outer shell layer. Synthetic fibers such as polyester don't absorb water when wet and retain most of their insulating ability. In wet weather, avoid cotton, which absorbs water like a sponge and dries very slowly. Rescue teams have a saying: "Cotton kills."

Water Purification

On day outings, you should carry all the water you'll need. Backpackers who have to use backcountry water sources such as springs, natural tanks, and streams should always purify or filter all water before use. Purifiers, which include halide chemicals, some filter-based devices, and ultraviolet light units, remove viruses as well as bacteria and cysts. Most filters do not remove viruses, but luckily virus-borne diseases are uncommon in this area. Filters improve the taste of the water, but are slow, heavy, and bulky compared with chemical purifiers. Keep filters clean by replacing the filter element or cleaning it as per the manufacturer's instructions.

When using chemical purifying agents, follow the instructions carefully, especially in regard to the wait time for the chemical to complete its work. Never add flavored drink mixes to water until the wait time has elapsed, because the ascorbic acid (vitamin C) used in many drink mixes neutralizes the purifying agent.

Bringing water to a boil purifies it at any altitude, but it uses a lot of fuel and leaves you with a hot, flat-tasting drink. Pouring boiled water back and forth between two pots cools it off and restores the dissolved air that makes water taste better.

Altitude Sickness

Climbers ascending Mount Shasta are commonly affected by altitude sickness, which is caused by the decreasing amount of oxygen available at higher elevations. Symptoms include nausea, weakness, headache, loss of appetite, shortness of breath, and difficulty in sleeping. Resting and eating high-energy foods and drinking water will usually help, but if symptoms become worse, the only cure is to descend to lower elevations. In rare cases, pulmonary edema may develop, marked by a rapid deterioration in the victim and fluid in the lungs. Only a rapid descent to a lower altitude will save the victim's life.

Poison Oak

Poison oak is common up to about the 5,000-foot elevation, where it's often but not always associated with the more common wild grape. The organic acid in the sap of poison oak causes a skin irritation in many people. Learn to recognize poison oak's distinctive glossy leaves, which always grow in groups of three. If you suspect you've been exposed, wash the affected area with soap and water, or just plain water, as soon as possible. Remember that dogs and pant legs can carry the sap to human skin as well. Calamine lotion is best for relieving the itching. Serious cases may require medical attention.

Animal Hazards

Rattlesnakes can be found at the lower elevations and, rarely, as high as timberline. Rattlesnakes are not aggressive and go out of their way to avoid an encounter. They usually sense your presence before you are aware of them and move quietly out of the way. If an intruder does get too close, or the snake is surprised or cornered, it uses its rattle as a warning well before you come in range of its strike.

The rattling sound, which the snake creates by rapidly shaking the rattle on its tail, is an unmistakable sound but one that can be difficult to locate, especially in grass or brush. When you first hear it, stop and locate the snake visually before moving quietly around it. Snakes sometimes den up together, so watch for other snakes as you avoid the first one. Never handle or tease any snake. Most snakebite victims are snake collectors, people working around rock or woodpiles, and people playing with snakes.

Since rattlesnakes can strike no farther than approximately half their body length, avoid placing your hands and feet in areas that you cannot see, and walk several feet away from rock overhangs and shady ledges. Bites usually occur on the feet or ankles, so ankle-high hiking boots and loose-fitting long pants will prevent most injuries. Snakes prefer surfaces at about 80 degrees Fahrenheit. This means they like the shade of bushes or rock overhangs in hot weather, and in cool weather they prefer open, sunny ground. Don't confuse commonly found but nonpoisonous bull snakes with rattlesnakes: Bull snakes don't have rattles on their tails.

Although rattlesnake bites are not life threatening except in rare cases usually involving the very young or infirm, the venom can do serious damage to tis-

Poison oak.

sue. Since the snake's venom is designed to immobilize mice and other small mammals, which are the rattlesnake's usual prey, a rattlesnake usually saves its venom for hunting strikes. Warning bites often inject little or no venom. Actually, the main hazards from most accidental rattlesnake bites are panic on the part of the victim and infection caused by the deep puncture wounds. If someone does get bitten, keep the victim calm and transport him or her to medical care as soon as possible. If possible, identify the snake, but not at the risk of further bites. Rattlesnake bites can be identified by the two puncture marks from the venom-injecting fangs, in addition to teeth marks. Nonvenomous snakes can certainly bite you but do not leave fang marks.

Mountain lions (also known as pumas or cougars) roam the mountains and are occasionally sighted. More often, you'll just see their tracks. There have been a few lion attacks on mountain bikers and runners, where the big cats have apparently reacted to fast-moving humans as prey. Lions attack deer, their normal prey, by ambush and will not attack if at a disadvantage or outnumbered.

That means that groups are safer than solo hikers. It also means you should make yourself appear as large as possible if you encounter a lion, by standing up straight, spreading your jacket wide, and so on. Experts advise that you avoid eye contact and move away slowly. If attacked, fight back with anything at hand. Many lion encounters involve roaming dogs, so keep dogs on a leash.

Although grizzly bears have long been extinct in California, black bears are common. Their color may range from black to brown or cinnamon. While black bears are naturally shy of humans, they are curious and are attracted to food and garbage odors. To avoid problems with bears, never cook in your tent or around your sleeping bag. In the backcountry, use a long piece of nylon cord and a rock to hang your food, trash, and all items with an odor such as sunscreen, insect repellent, lotions, toothpaste, and trash from a tree limb too weak to support a bear, well above the ground and well away from the trunk. A bear-proof Kevlar food sack or plastic canister greatly improves the odds of keeping bears out of your food. In campgrounds, stash all food, trash, and toiletries in bear-proof boxes, if provided, or out of sight in your vehicle. Bears know what coolers contain and will break into a vehicle to get at them. Remember that your main goal is to keep the bears from getting the idea that campers are a meal ticket, not to protect your food supply for yourself. The worst case for you is that you'll have to abort your trip; the worst case for a bear is that it becomes a persistent nuisance and injures or threatens to injure someone, in which case wildlife managers are left with no choice but to kill the bear.

Raccoons, skunks, mice, and other rodents are nocturnal animals that often become camp robbers, especially at heavily used campsites. All of them are persistent and can easily ruin your night's sleep. A bear-proof campsite box or portable bear-proof plastic container solves the problem, and a Kevlar bear sack at least slows them down. Food left in a vehicle is not safe from mice, as I found out the hard way when mice chewed their way through the ventilation ducts in my car, which was parked at a trailhead for several days with a plastic bag of tasty nuts sitting on the center console. When backpacking, hang your food if possible, and leave all pack pockets open so rodents can explore the enticing residual smells without having to chew their way in.

Mosquitoes are usually around in small numbers until the first hard freezes in the fall, and are numerous during the first few weeks after snowmelt. Because mosquitoes can transmit West Nile virus, use repellent and sleep in a tent when they are present. DEET in various concentrations seems to be the most effective repellent, though several newer and less unpleasant repellents based on picaridin and citronella are coming on the market.

Ticks are common in some places in the Shasta region, especially at lower elevations and along streams and rivers. Since ticks can carry Lyme disease, it is important to find and remove them from your skin before they become embedded. In tick-prone areas, inspect all of your skin at least once a day, and remove any ticks by gently pulling. Wearing long pants and applying DEET-based insect repellents to pant legs and socks can help keep ticks off.

History

Natives

When Europeans first discovered the Shasta region, several native tribes had already been calling the area home for thousands of years. These included the Shasta Indians north of Mount Shasta, the Modocs to the east of the mountain, and the Wintu to the south. The rivers and streams of the region provided a relatively easy living for these hunter-gatherers. The waters provided salmon and other fish, while the lush valleys and surrounding forests were full of deer, elk, and other game animals, as well as numerous food and medicinal plants. Native peoples lived in the low-elevation river valleys, which have a mild climate year-round, and made occasional forays into the high country only during the summer, to follow game or trade routes. Though all travel was on foot, the tribes traded among themselves and with tribes farther away. For example, obsidian from the Modoc area east of Mount Shasta was widely prized because the glassy volcanic rock made good arrowheads and spear points. Unfortunately, the arrival of Europeans brought an end to the natives' relatively easy life. Not only did the newcomers claim large tracts of land for themselves, but they also hunted the game and fur-bearing animals, and far worse, inadvertently introduced deadly diseases such as smallpox to which the locals had no immunity. Inevitably, such pressures created conflicts between the natives and the invaders, and several battles were fought in the Shasta region between the U.S. Army and local tribes.

Early Explorers

The Spanish and the Russians were the first to settle the northern California region, both arriving by sea. Spain explored the Baja California coast and the American Southwest in the 1540s and established forts and settlements soon after, but they didn't succeed in establishing outposts in California until the late eighteenth century. By the time the Mexican Revolution wrested control of the area from Spain in 1821, there were settlements along the coast and inland from San Francisco southward.

About this time, the Russians, expanding their New World colonies south from Alaska, established Fort Ross on the coast about sixty miles northwest of San Francisco Bay. Meanwhile, English fur trappers and the Hudson Bay

Company were establishing a strong presence in British Columbia and the American Northwest. One of the Hudson Bay Company trappers traveled through central Oregon in 1827 and may have seen Mount Shasta.

Gold Rush Fever

California was ceded to the United States in 1848 as a result of the Mexican-American War. Gold was discovered on the Sacramento River in 1849, and the gold rush soon moved north and west into the Shasta country. Although little gold was found in the volcanic rocks around Mount Shasta itself, the Trinity River and its tributaries were heavily mined for placer gold. These small-scale mining operations did little damage to the forests and streams, but when the placer gold ran out, large corporations moved in with giant hydraulic machines that used high-pressure streams of water to wash away entire mountainsides. The effects of this mining activity are still visible today in the form of huge piles of rock left when the waste rock was dumped in stream- and riverbeds.

Ranchers and Settlers

The waves of miners were followed by American settlers, and by the end of the 1850s numerous ranches and small settlements had been established in the Shasta country, mainly along the hospitable river valleys. The country became more accessible when the railroad pushed north from Redding to the town of Mount Shasta in 1886. The railroad made timber production possible on a large scale.

Forest Reserve to National Forest

Concerned that western forests were being overcut and would disappear like the eastern forests, in 1899 President Theodore Roosevelt used his powers under the Antiquities Act to set aside large portions of the western forests as national forest reserves. This system of public lands set aside for conservation was formalized by Congress when it created the present national forest system in 1905, along with an agency, the U.S. Forest Service, to manage the forests. Early forest rangers were responsible for immense tracts of land and had to be skilled horsemen, foresters, and firefighters, as well as administrators.

The U.S. Forest Service, created to manage the national forests for multiple uses, and the National Park Service, created in 1916 to manage the national parks primarily for preservation, were part of the growing conservation movement that had many of its roots in California. The present Shasta–Trinity National Forest was created from the previous forest reserve as two separate national forests, the Shasta and the Trinity, and then later combined into one forest.

Preservationists within the U.S. Forest Service convinced the agency to protect some of the roadless areas in the national forests, and this arrangement was formalized in 1964 with the signing of the act creating the National Wilderness

Preservation System, which recognized that some tracts of public land should be preserved in a wilderness state without any permanent human presence. Most of the existing wilderness areas within the national forests became congressionally protected wilderness areas, and many other roadless areas, including the Trinity Alps, Castle Crags, and Mount Shasta, have been added to the wilderness system since then.

The vast Central Valley, lying between the coast ranges and the Sierra Nevada, is the most productive farmland on the planet, and as such has an insatiable demand for water. Southern portions of the valley in particular needed more water, and in the 1960s several large dams were built on the Trinity and Sacramento Rivers to store and divert water to these thirsty areas. Recognizing the recreational potential of these huge artificial lakes set in such scenic country, Congress created the Whiskeytown–Shasta–Trinity National Recreation Area (NRA) to develop and manage recreational sites along the reservoirs. The U.S. Forest Service manages the Shasta and Trinity Units of the NRA, while the National Park Service manages the Whiskeytown Unit.

Natural History

In the Shasta region, the major mountain ranges west of the Trinity River are the Salmon Mountains, Trinity Alps, and Scott Mountains. These are all subranges of the Klamath Mountains. The crest of these ranges wanders south, then east, then northeast, before turning southeast. Between the Trinity and Sacramento Rivers, the Trinity Mountains run in a generally north-south alignment, flanked by Trinity Reservoir on the Trinity River and Shasta Lake on the Sacramento River. Castle Crags, a small but rugged range, rises abruptly west of the upper Sacramento River and runs generally east-west. All these ranges are rugged, with steep slopes, glacier-carved peaks, sparkling alpine lakes, and deep, forested canyons.

Geology and Geography

The complex topography of the Klamath Mountains reflects their complicated geology, which has resulted from the collision of the Pacific and North American plates. The earth's surface is made up of seven major and several minor plates of rock, which float on the semiliquid mantle below. Continental plates are about 25 miles thick and are made up of lightweight and light-colored granitic rocks, in contrast to oceanic plates, which are about 6 miles thick and composed of heavier, dark basaltic rocks. The plates are constantly on the move, riding on slow currents in the mantle like ice floes in a polar sea. When the plates collide, the margins crumple and are forced upward into mountain ranges and downward to become deeply buried. Bits and pieces of each plate may scrape off onto the other plate.

Castle Lake.

Rocks that become deeply buried by plate collision are modified by the extreme heat and pressure found miles below the surface. Even though not melted, the minerals in the original volcanic and sedimentary rocks are modified enough to create new, metamorphic rocks. Later, when the metamorphic rocks are lifted upward into mountain ranges such as the Klamath Mountains, complex folding and faulting further mask the origins of the rocks.

Recent geologic evidence shows that the formation of the Klamath Mountains also involved accretion. Small pieces of continental crust—microcontinents like the Japanese Islands—have been carried to the west coast of North America by the eastward movement of the Pacific plate, there to lodge against the North American plate. Over millions of years, many such microcontinents have accreted on the edge of the North American plate to build up the coastal mountains and the Klamath Mountains.

The Sacramento River marks the divide between the Klamath Mountains and the Cascade Mountains, an inland range that starts at Mount Lassen on the south and continues northward past Mount Shasta to include the inland mountains of Oregon and Washington and southern British Columbia. The southern Cascades are volcanic mountains and are also a result of plate collision.

When a heavier oceanic plate like the Pacific plate collides with a lighter continental plate such as the North American plate, the oceanic plate dives, or subducts, beneath the continental plate. When the oceanic plate reaches a depth of about 60 miles, it melts and becomes part of the mantle. As the top surface of the diving plate rubs and scrapes along the underneath of the continental plate, friction heats and melts the rock, creating pockets of magma. When magma finds a weakness in the continental plate above, it may make its way to the surface, erupting as lava.

Lava and cinders blasted from volcanic vents sometimes pile up to form huge, symmetrical stratovolcanoes such as Mount Shasta. Or, depending on the composition of the lava, it may spread out into lava flows that cover hundreds of square miles. The Cascades were created by the accumulation of lava and other volcanic rocks, rather than by faulting and uplift as in the Klamath Mountains. Most of the Cascade volcanoes are very young as geologic time goes, having been created in the last million years. Steam vents and other activity on many of the volcanoes show that the Cascades are still active. The explosive eruptions of Mount Lassen in 1914 and Mount St. Helens in 1980 prove beyond a doubt that the Cascade volcanoes are still active. They also provide a natural laboratory for studying volcanic eruptions and recovery of forests devastated by the volcanoes.

While most of the landscape in the Shasta region was eroded to its present form by water, a process that continues, the highest peaks were sculpted by glaciers. Although Mount Shasta is the only mountain in the region to have glaciers at present, evidence of past glaciers is found on the highest summits in the Trinity Alps and a few other peaks. As recently as 10,000 years ago, yearly snowfall on the highest peaks exceeded the rate at which it melted, and so permanent icefields formed. As the layers of ice grew deeper, they began to move downhill under their own weight, becoming a river of ice—a glacier.

Just as a riverbed has a U-shaped profile, so does a glacier's bed, except that a glacier can fill an entire valley. A U-shaped profile is clear evidence that the valley was once filled with a glacier. Where water plunges over a cliff or down a steep slope, it can carve out a plunge pool at the bottom of its fall. Glaciers produce basins near their heads, where snow accumulates at the greatest rate. After the glaciers melt, the basins at their head often fill with meltwater, creating tarns, or classic alpine lakes. Also, the heads of glaciers pluck away aggressively at the mountain slopes above them, making them steeper and creating mountains with high, near-vertical walls and sharp summits. The high summits of the Trinity Alps were carved by such glaciers, and glacial ice continues to pluck away at Mount Shasta.

Trees of the Shasta Region

Because of the confluence of Rocky Mountain, Sierra Nevada, Cascade, and coastal forest types in the Shasta region, these vast forests are among the most diverse on earth. There are many different species of trees, including both coniferous trees, which are evergreen and keep their needles or leaves throughout the year, and deciduous trees, which lose their leaves each fall and grow new ones in the spring.

Gray pines, odd-shaped trees with branches growing at strange angles, have three long needles growing in a stiff bunch, with edible nuts within the scales of its cone. These nuts were an important food source for natives, and squirrels and birds still depend on them.

Lodgepole pines favor middle and higher elevations in the region and were much sought after for construction by both natives and pioneers because they grow straight and tall, with a very gradual taper to the trunk. The short needles grow in bunches of two and form dense clusters on the ends of branches, which gives the branches the appearance of a bottlebrush. Lodgepole pines actually depend on fire to reproduce. The cones are resinous, which prevents squirrels and birds from easily getting at the seeds. Heat from a forest fire melts the resin and frees the seeds, which fall on freshly burned ground clear of competing plants and covered with nutrient-rich ash.

Knobcone pines favor warmer, south-facing slopes and have three long yellowish green needles per bunch. Like lodgepole pines, knobcone pines depend on fire to release their seeds from the cones.

Ponderosa pines are large pines with long, dark green needles in groups of three. Ponderosas grow over 150 feet in height, and older trees are marked by orange- to cinnamon-colored bark that flakes off in puzzle-shaped pieces. The flaky bark gives the ponderosa exceptional resistance to fire, as it insulates the living tree from a wildfire running up the outer bark. Ponderosa pines are very heat tolerant, and they grow on lower, hotter slopes in the Shasta region more than any other large tree. Ponderosas are not as cold tolerant as other conifers, though, which limits their upper range.

After ponderosa pines, Douglas fir is the next most heat-tolerant tree, and it typically grows at higher elevations than the ponderosa and on cooler, north-facing slopes, mixing with ponderosas at the lower limits of its range. Technically, the Douglas fir is not a true fir. The cones hang down from the branches, but those of true firs grow upward. The short needles are flat (as opposed to square in cross section like the spruces) and grow in all directions from the branches. Deeply furrowed, the bark is resistant to fire and is gray or sometimes reddish brown.

Sugar pines are the tallest pine in the world, often reaching over 200 feet tall and 6 feet in diameter. The cones are very large, often reaching a foot in length. Blue-green needles, about 3 inches long, grow in a bunch of five, and the bark is light brown or gray, consisting of alternating furrows and scaly ridges. Sugar pine gets its name from the sugary taste of its resin.

Shasta red fir, a true fir, is common at high elevations in the Shasta region. The short, stiff needles curve upward from the branches. Old-growth red firs have furrowed, reddish brown bark. The cones, which grow upright on the branches near the crown of the tree, fall apart in place, leaving the stem standing upright.

White fir grows throughout the Shasta region. The cones are smaller than those of the red fir and not as shaggy in appearance. At lower elevations, white fir needles tend to grow horizontally from the branches, but at higher altitudes the needles tend to curve upward from the branches.

Foxtail pines have five short, stiff needles per bunch and grow near timberline. Deep cold tends to kill buds and branches exposed to the wind, and wind-driven snow erodes and kills needles and bark, which forces foxtail pines into strange shapes. A strip of bark on the lee side of the trunk may be the only thing keeping the tree alive. Living in such a harsh environment, foxtail pines grow very slowly, and even a small tree can be more than 2,000 years old.

Another tree found at the upper limit of trees is the whitebark pine. This alpine tree is very adaptable to its environment, growing as tall, slender trees in protected locations, and hugging the ground and filling the space behind boulders in exposed locations at the very upper limit of tree growth. Such misshaped timberline trees are called "krumholtz," regardless of the tree species. In

Ponderosa pine, Pacific Crest National Scenic Trail.

slightly more protected locations, whitebark pines grow in "tree islands," tight groups of pines growing together for mutual protection from the cold and wind.

Western white pines grow over 110 feet tall and can reach 175 feet. The blue-green, 2- to 3-inch needles grow in bunches of five, and the relatively short branches of the tree form an open crown. The bark is silver-gray, and the long, slender cones are smaller than those of the sugar pine. Western white pine favors high-elevation forests, where snow lingers well into summer, ensuring a supply of water.

Incense cedar is named for its distinctive smell, which most people are familiar with because the wood is commonly used to make pencils. The tree commonly grows to 150 feet. The needles resemble those of a juniper tree, growing in whorls of four from flattened branches. On old-growth trees, the bark is dark brown to red, fibrous, with deep, irregular furrows.

Port Orford cedar resembles incense cedar, but the branches are not as flattened. Younger trees have reddish brown, vertically ridged bark, which becomes fibrous silver-brown on mature trees.

Pacific yew grows as high as 75 feet and favors shaded, moist areas along streams. The needles are flat and prickly tipped, emerge horizontally from the branches, and are dark green on top and light green underneath. Reddish purple bark peels off to reveal a soft, rose-colored inner bark. The berries are salmon-colored. Yew was much prized by Native Americans for bows.

Mountain hemlock is a high-altitude tree, associated with red fir. Its stiff branches help the tree shed snow, and the bark is a combination of soft purples, silvers, and grays. The wood is tough, and dead trees often stand for hundreds of years. Small, bright purple cones crowding the top of the tree are often dripping with pitch.

An uncommon high-altitude tree is the weeping spruce, which has long, slender branches that sometimes droop all the way to the ground. Silver-green needles emerge from all sides of the branches.

Big-leafed maple, appropriately enough, has the largest leaves of any tree in the Shasta region. The five-lobed leaves are up to a foot across and turn bright yellow in the fall. Falling seeds spin on double wings as they float to the ground. The presence of this tree often indicates high amounts of groundwater.

Vine maple prefers deeply shaded, moist canyons and is vinelike in appearance. The leaves are large and papery, turning lemon yellow in the fall. Seeds are similar to that of the big-leafed maple. The bark is greenish with shallow white furrows.

Black oak is a deciduous oak, with dark green, deeply lobed leaves with a prickle on the tip of each lobe. Ridges and furrows mark the dark bark. Acorns from the black oak were a staple food of Native Americans throughout the area.

As the name implies, canyon live oak is evergreen, keeping its thick, leathery leaves all year. Leaves may be rounded or toothed, even on the same tree, and are bright green on top and tawny brown underneath. Easily damaged by fire, the bark is dark, scaly, and ridged. Canyon live oak prefers cool, rocky drainages.

Tan oak is not a true oak, being related to the chestnut. Leaves are dark green on top, lighter on the bottom, and the underside is covered with a snowy white wool-like fuzz. The bark is ridged and was once used for tanning hides.

Sadler oak prefers open, rocky slopes at middle elevations. Light green leaves are broad and toothed, and the acorns are important to deer.

Blue oak grows in low-elevation woodlands, on dry flats and slopes. The smooth-edged and wavy leaves are a light bluish green on top and a paler bluish green underneath, and the bark is light colored and papery feeling.

A common, low-elevation streamside tree is black cottonwood. On top, the leaves are dark green, while underneath they are silvery white. In the fall, black cottonwood turns bright yellow.

Quaking aspen has white bark. The leaves, dark green on top and silvery underneath, are on long, slender stems, which allow them to flutter in light winds, giving the entire tree a shimmering appearance. In the Shasta region, aspens grow in small pockets and are not common.

Pacific madrone is a large and beautiful tree with smooth, reddish brown bark, which is rough and deeply furrowed on older trees. The evergreen leaves are shiny, deep green on top and yellow-green underneath. Large, showy flowers grow in clusters.

Pacific (or mountain) dogwood prefers cool, shady drainages and areas that are well watered. The large, saucer-shaped flower clusters appear in late April at lower elevations and in June at higher locations. Veins and a point at the tip mark the leaves, which turn bright red in the fall. The bark looks like an alligator's hide and is gray to black in color.

McNab cypress prefers dry slopes and flats and is found with manzanita and pine/oak woodlands. This low-growing tree has long branches covered with short, gray to blue-green needles. The dark brown bark is fibrous.

Barely reaching tree height, California juniper grows on sage flats and sometimes with piñon pine. The bark is thin and dark gray, and the cones, often called juniper berries, are round and gray-blue when young, red-brown when mature.

One easy way to tell if a tree is a pine, fir, or spruce is to pluck a needle. Nearly all pines have needles that grow in groups of two or more. Spruce and fir needles grow singly, but spruce needles are squarish in cross section, while fir needles are flattened. If the needle rolls easily between your fingers, it came from a spruce, and if not, it's from a fir. Singleleaf piñon pine is the only common pine with needles that grow singly, and it is found at lower elevations than spruce and fir.

Shasta–Trinity National Forest

Getting to the Forest

Air and bus service is available to Redding, the gateway city located on Interstate 5 at the southern edge of the Shasta country. Once there, you'll need a car to explore the region since there is no public transport.

Getting around the Forest

Interstate 5 is California's main north-south highway, and it bisects the Shasta–Trinity National Forest, running north from Redding, crossing the Pit River and Sacramento River arms of Shasta Lake in two places. I–5 then follows the Sacramento River north to the town of Dunsmuir, then loosely follows the Shasta River past the town of Mount Shasta, around the west side of Mount Shasta, and on north through the town of Yreka before heading into Oregon. I–5 and paved and gravel side roads are the primary access routes to Shasta Lake and Castle Crags.

Highway 299 runs west from Redding past Whiskeytown Lake, through the town of Weaverville, then follows the Trinity River along the south side of the Trinity Alps. Highway 299 is the main access to the Whiskeytown Unit of the Whiskeytown–Shasta–Trinity National Recreation Area, the Trinity River, and forest roads leading to trailheads along the southern edge of the Trinity Alps.

At Weaverville, Highway 3 heads north along the west side of Trinity Lake, eventually climbing over Scott Pass and crossing the Pacific Crest National Scenic Trail before descending to Yreka and meeting I–5. Highway 3 is the main access to Lewiston and Trinity Lakes. Numerous forest roads lead west to trailheads along the east side of the Trinity Alps.

Just south of Scott Pass, Forest Road 17 forks northeast and climbs over Parks Pass before descending to meet I–5 northwest of the town of Mount Shasta. Forest Road 17 provides access to the Pacific Crest Trail at Parks Pass.

Highway 89 runs east from the town of Mount Shasta and I–5 through the town of McCloud and eventually southeast to Lassen Volcanic National Park.

The highway provides access to the McCloud River area, and forest roads lead to trailheads on the south and east sides of Mount Shasta. Forest Road 15 runs north from Highway 89 and is the main access to the Modoc volcanic highlands east of Mount Shasta.

Whiskeytown Lake Unit: Whiskeytown–Shasta–Trinity National Recreation Area

Whiskeytown Lake lies in the steep, rugged Klamath Mountains, an area characterized by wet winters and dry summers. The combination of heavy precipitation and frequent wildfires has created an exceptionally diverse landscape, from chaparral brushlands and oak woodlands to pine-fir forests.

The Whiskeytown Unit's main attraction is Whiskeytown Lake, a reservoir with a 36-mile shoreline covering 3,200 acres. Part of the Central Valley Project, Whiskeytown Lake's purpose is to divert water from the Trinity River watershed to the Sacramento River, as part of the project's overall mission of moving water from northern California to the rich agriculture areas of the Central Valley. Scenery around the lake is exceptional, from the forested shoreline to the mountains towering above the lake. The lake normally stays full all summer and is at an elevation of 1,200 feet. Whiskeytown Lake is especially popular with sailors, paddlers, and windsurfers, but powerboaters, water-skiers, anglers, scuba divers, and swimmers all make good use of the area.

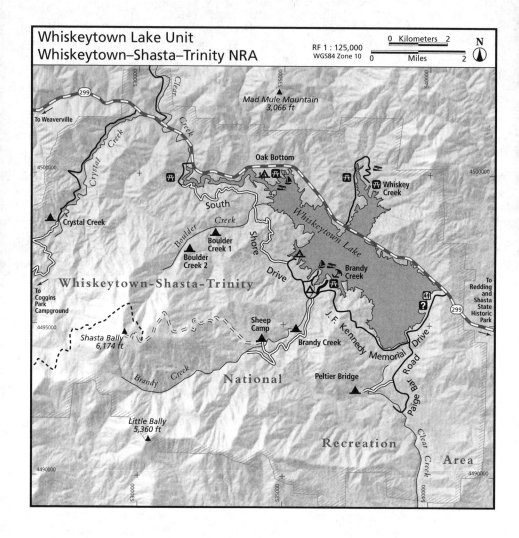

Whiskeytown also includes 39,000 acres of public land surrounding the lake. Permanent streams and miles of hiking trails appeal to those who want to camp, pan for gold, watch birds, ride horses, mountain bike, engage in photography, or drive a scenic road.

A pass must be obtained at the visitor center and displayed on your dashboard. Daily, weekly, and annual passes are available for a fee. Holders of National Parks, Golden Eagle, Gold Age, and Gold Access Passes are admitted free.

Visitor Centers and Amenities

The Whiskeytown Visitor Center is 8 miles west of Redding on Highway 299, at the J. F. Kennedy Memorial Drive turnoff and the east end of Whiskeytown Lake. The city of Redding is the nearest supply point. Brandy Creek Marina is located near the west end of J. F. Kennedy Memorial Drive on the south shore of the lake and has a small store during the summer. Oak Bottom Marina is on Highway 299 near the west end of the lake and has a small store and boat rentals during the summer.

Campgrounds

Oak Bottom Campground, off Highway 299 near the west end of the lake, has two units: a tent campground with restrooms, and an RV campground with restrooms, a dump station, and water but no hookups. Showers are available at the Oak Bottom Beach restrooms.

Brandy Creek RV Campground, on J. F. Kennedy Memorial Drive on the south shore of the lake, has restrooms and water but no hookups.

In addition, there are several primitive campgrounds located in the backcountry. These have tables, fire rings, food storage lockers, and restrooms. Peltier Bridge Campground and Horse Camp are reached via J. F. Kennedy Memorial Drive and Paige Bar Road. Brandy Creek Campground and Sheep Camp are reached via J. F. Kennedy Memorial Drive and the Brandy Creek Road. Crystal Creek and Coggins Park Campgrounds are reached from the Crystal Creek Road. Boulder Creek 1 and Boulder Creek 2 are reached via the Boulder Creek Trail.

A fee is required for use of the campgrounds, and there is a fourteen-day stay limit from May 15 through September 15, a thirty-day stay limit during the rest of the year.

Historic Sites

The Tower House Historic District is located in the northwest corner of the Whiskeytown Unit, on Highway 299. The historic district preserves some of the efforts of partners Charles Camden and Levi Tower, who came to the Whiskeytown gold rush area in 1850, eager to find success. Tower started a thriving luxury hotel, the Tower House, while Camden mined gold and built a sawmill, water ditches, and toll roads and bridges. The Camden House remains today as a reminder of these early entrepreneurs.

Scenic Drives

From the visitor center, Highway 299 runs along the north shore of the lake, offering scenic views. Along the way, this state highway crosses the Whiskey

Creek arm of the lake on a bridge, and passes the turnoffs to the Whiskey Creek and Oak Bottom recreation sites, as well as the Tower House Historic District. The one-way driving distance is 9 miles.

Also starting from the visitor center, the J. F. Kennedy Memorial Drive heads south and west around the lake, crossing Whiskeytown Dam and the Brandy Creek recreation sites before ending at Dry Creek Group Campground. The total distance is 5 miles.

Another scenic, paved road is the Crystal Creek Road, which leaves Highway 299 at the west end of the Whiskeytown Unit, just west of the Tower House Historic District. This 4-mile road winds south along Crystal Creek, passing Crystal Creek Falls and picnic area, as well as Crystal Creek Campground.

Whiskeytown Lake is popular with sailors and paddlers.

Fishing

Whiskeytown Lake can be fished from shore or a boat. Species in the lake include rainbow and brown trout, largemouth, smallmouth, and spotted bass, and kokanee salmon. The California Department of Fish and Game regulates fishing, and a valid fishing license is required. Ask at the visitor center for information on restrictions in the Whiskeytown Unit.

Water Sports

Whiskeytown Lake offers canoeing, kayaking, swimming, powerboating, sailing, windsurfing, and water-skiing. Personal watercraft, such as Jet Skis, are prohibited on Whiskeytown Lake. Boat ramps are located at Brandy Creek and Oak Bottom Marinas, and at Whiskey Creek, located north of Highway 299 on the north shore of the lake. California and federal boating laws apply.

Trails

Other than the entry fee, no permit is required for day hiking and mountain biking. Backpackers must have a backcountry camping permit, obtainable at the visitor center.

Mount Shasta Mine

HIGHLIGHTS: Vistas of Whiskeytown Lake and Orofino Gulch, historic gold mines, and spring wildflower displays (best in late March).

TYPE OF TRIP: Loop.

DISTANCE: 2.4 miles.

DIFFICULTY: Moderate.

PERMITTED USES: Hiking, mountain biking, horses.

MAPS: Whiskeytown–Shasta–Trinity National Recreation Area Topographic Map (Earthwalk Press), Igo (USGS).

SPECIAL CONSIDERATIONS: During the hot summer months, take plenty of drinking water. The creek is not safe to drink. Poison oak is abundant along the trail. Do not enter any mine shaft.

PARKING AND FACILITIES: Parking lot and restroom.

FINDING THE TRAILHEAD: From the visitor center on Highway 299, drive south 1 mile on J. F. Kennedy Memorial Drive. Just before crossing Whiskeytown Dam, stay left on Paige Bar Road, and continue 1.2 miles to the Mount Shasta Mine Trailhead, on the left, across from Peltier Valley Road.

The trail can be hiked or ridden in either direction; this description is counterclockwise. From the Mount Shasta Mine Trailhead, the trail traverses an area burned by prescribed fires in 2002 and 2004. Prescribed fires are used to remove excess fuel from the forest floor and to simulate the conditions created by natural fires.

Relatively level, the first section of the trail runs through a forest of canyon live oaks and knobcone pines. Poison oak, manzanita, and blueblossom ceanothus make up most of the brush cover.

Whiskeytown Cemetery is visible on the right. This cemetery was built when the original was flooded by the creation of Whiskeytown Lake in 1963. Farther on, the trail crosses the Great Water Ditch Trail several times. This trail follows the bed of a 40-mile ditch finished in 1855, which carried water to gold mines farther south.

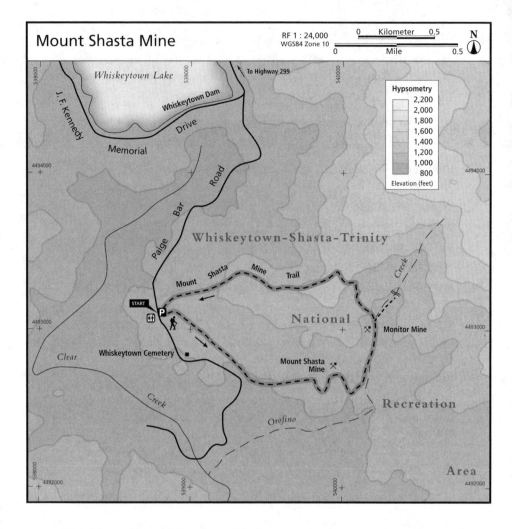

The Mount Shasta Mine Loop Trail passes a large canyon live oak near the Mount Shasta Mine. Originally opened in 1897, the mine was sold the same year for $10,000. Over the next fourteen years the mine was greatly expanded and produced about $178,000 from quartz ore. At first, the ore was hauled to the Keswick smelter for processing, but around 1900, the owners built a steam-powered stamp mill capable of crushing 50 tons of rock per day. A sign at the mine explains the Mount Shasta Mine in more detail.

One geological theory holds that the Mount Shasta Mine is located in the remnant of an ancient magma chamber, which fed volcanic action 400 million years ago that created offshore islands near the ancient coastline. The original basalt has been metamorphosed into a rock called the Copley greenstone. Later vulcanism liquified minerals with low melting points, and high pressure injected the melted rock into fractures in the surrounding rock. Gold and quartz were injected together into the rock and later exposed at Orofino Gulch. Since quartz and gold are often found together, miners are attracted to quartz outcrops. One hundred years ago, a half dozen gold mines were in operation along Orofino Gulch.

To the left, just past the mine and behind a huge greenstone boulder, is a meadow that is often spectacular with yellow monkeyflowers and blue dicks during late March. Now the trail skirts Orofino Creek, passes the Monitor Mine, and follows Orofino Creek upstream. A right fork in the trail leads 100 feet to a fine waterfall and pool, flowing during the spring.

The main Mount Shasta Mine Trail continues up Orofino Creek past spring wildflowers, including buttercups, shooting stars, pussy ears, and Indian warriors. A mine shaft on the left is gated to allow bats and other wildlife to pass through while keeping people out.

Now the trail turns northwest and starts a steady climb through black, blue, and canyon live oaks and knobcone and ponderosa pines. Across the canyon, you can see Kanaka Peak, South Fork Mountain, and Shasta Bally (6,174 feet).

At the high point the trail crosses the Orofino fuel break road and offers views of Whiskeytown Dam, the lake, and, in the distance, the Trinity Mountains. The trail now descends southwest to complete the loop at the Mount Shasta Mine Trailhead.

KEY POINTS

0.0 Mount Shasta Mine Trailhead.

0.2 Whiskeytown Cemetery.

0.9 Mount Shasta Mine.

1.4 Monitor Mine.

2.4 Mount Shasta Mine Trailhead.

Boulder Creek Trail

HIGHLIGHTS: A multiuse trail to 81-foot Boulder Creek Falls.

TYPE OF TRIP: Out-and-back.

DISTANCE: 6.6 miles.

DIFFICULTY: Moderate.

PERMITTED USES: Hiking, mountain biking, horseback riding.

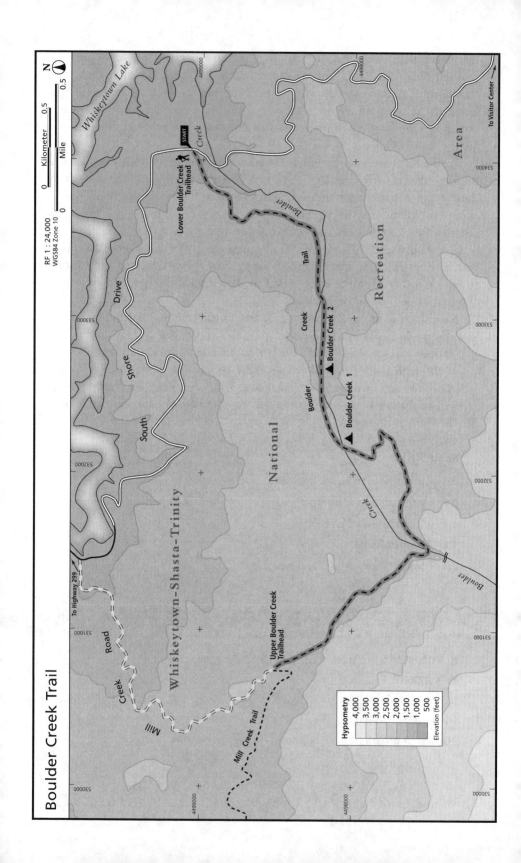

Boulder Creek Trail

RF 1 : 24,000
WGS84 Zone 10

N

Kilometer		0.5
0		

Mile		0.5
0		

Whiskeytown Lake

Lower Boulder Creek Trailhead

START

Creek

South Shore Drive

To Highway 299

Mill Creek Road

Mill Creek Trail

Upper Boulder Creek Trailhead

Whiskeytown-Shasta-Trinity

National

Recreation

Area

Boulder

Creek

Trail

Boulder Creek 1

Boulder Creek 2

Boulder Creek

Boulder

To Visitor Center

Hypsometry

| 4,000 |
| 3,500 |
| 3,000 |
| 2,500 |
| 2,000 |
| 1,500 |
| 1,000 |
| 500 |

Elevation (feet)

MAPS: Whiskeytown–Shasta–Trinity National Recreation Area Topographic Map (Earthwalk Press), Whiskeytown (USGS), French Gulch (USGS).

SPECIAL CONSIDERATIONS: Poison oak is common along the trail. There are numerous stream crossings; watch for slippery rocks.

PARKING AND FACILITIES: Limited parking across the road from the trailhead.

FINDING THE TRAILHEAD: From the visitor center on Highway 299, drive 6.7 miles west on Highway 299, then turn left (south) on Carr Powerhouse Road, which becomes South Shore Drive at the powerhouse. The Lower Boulder Creek Trailhead is on the right, 3.4 miles from Highway 299.

For the first mile, the Boulder Creek Trail follows a former logging road though a thicket of knobcone pines and white leaf manzanita. Poison oak is common, as well as wild grape. As you near the creek, the brushland gradually gives way to a tall forest of ponderosa pines, Douglas fir, and canyon live oaks.

Now the Boulder Creek Trail follows Boulder Creek upstream, ultimately making four crossings. Sword and bracken ferns are very common in the moist environment created by the creek. At the third crossing, watch for the foundations of a residence last used in the 1960s. After the third crossing, the trail briefly climbs away from the creek to the south; turn right at a fork.

At the fourth and final crossing, a sign marks the short side trail to Boulder Creek Falls. There is a fine stand of big-leaf maples at the crossing. Boulder Creek Falls is 81 feet high, with a series of cascades above the falls adding another 28 feet of vertical drop.

After crossing the creek, the Boulder Creek Trail now heads north through a shady forest of black oaks, knobcone pines, and Douglas fir. Other common trees along this section of the trail include tan oaks, western dogwoods, and incense cedars. The trail ends at the Upper Boulder Creek Trailhead.

KEY POINTS

0.0 Lower Boulder Creek Trailhead.

1.0 Boulder Creek.

1.9 Stay right at a fork.

2.5 Trail leaves Boulder Creek to the north at the fourth creek crossing; short side trail to Boulder Creek Falls.

3.3 Upper Boulder Creek Trailhead and turnaround point.

Crystal Creek Water Ditch

HIGHLIGHTS: A shady, nearly level trail along Crystal Creek; first half wheelchair-accessible.

TYPE OF TRIP: Out-and-back.

DISTANCE: 1.6 miles.

DIFFICULTY: Easy.

PERMITTED USES: Hiking.

MAPS: Whiskeytown–Shasta–Trinity National Recreation Area Topographic Map (Earthwalk Press), French Gulch (USGS).

SPECIAL CONSIDERATIONS: Wheelchair-accessible for the first 0.4 mile of the trail.

PARKING AND FACILITIES: Dirt parking lot.

FINDING THE TRAILHEAD: From the visitor center on Highway 299, drive 8.5 miles west on Highway 299, then turn left (south) on Crystal Creek Road. Cross the bridge and drive 0.2 mile to the Crystal Creek Water Ditch Trailhead, on the left.

From the trailhead, the Crystal Creek Water Ditch Trail descends a short distance via two switchbacks, meeting the water ditch at the end of the second switchback. A cleanout house, added to the water ditch in 1913 by Charles Camden's daughter, uses an ingenious, water-powered rotary mechanism to remove pinecones and leaves from the water before it flows through a tunnel and under Highway 299 to Camden House.

From the cleanout house, the trail follows the water ditch as it contours along the hillside above Crystal Creek through a forest of canyon live oaks and ponderosa pines. You'll notice several drainage crossovers along the ditch. These carry seasonal runoff over the ditch so that it doesn't become flooded or washed out. Crystal Creek, which you've been hearing below you, becomes visible 0.2 mile from the trailhead.

At the halfway point, the hillside becomes too steep for a ditch, so a 250-foot trestle was built to support a flume to carry the water. The trail continues on a boardwalk with a handrail on the outside of the flume, but the boardwalk is too narrow for wheelchairs.

Beyond the trestle, the trail continues along the ditch. Although it may feel as though the trail and ditch descend gradually to the creek, this is an illusion. The ditch descends from the headworks, only at a lesser rate than the creek, so that water will flow down the ditch. As the trail reaches the creek, it becomes narrow and rocky, and some care is required to reach the actual headworks, where water from the creek is diverted into the ditch.

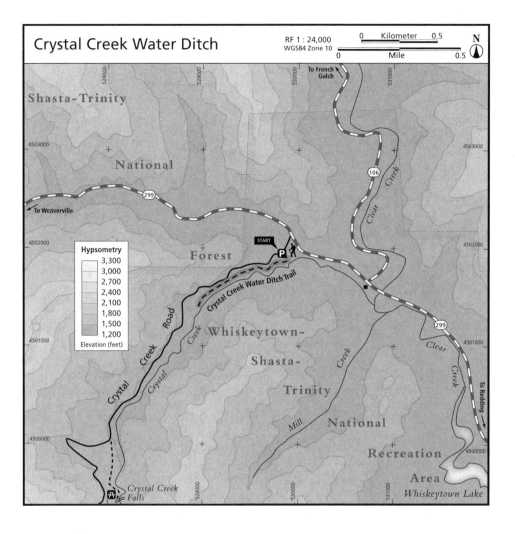

Crystal Creek Water Ditch

RF 1 : 24,000
WGS84 Zone 10

Collecting water from the creek to fill the ditch is not as simple as it might appear. A diversion dam across the creek pools the creek at just the right elevation for some water to enter the ditch, while allowing most of the flow to continue downstream in the creek. The concrete gate has a wooden baffle that can be raised or lowered to shut off the flow into the ditch. About 50 feet downstream, there is a wide section of the ditch that serves as a settling basin. The water slows down as it enters the side section, allowing silt and sand to settle out. Farther downstream along the ditch, there is a float that controls the level of the water and diverts excess water back to the creek. Next, the ditch goes through a tunnel cut through a rock buttress. A final structure appears to be the support for an undershot waterwheel, but the puzzle is what such a waterwheel would have powered, here on the creek.

Flume on Crystal Creek Water Ditch.

As the complexity of the headworks and the ditch shows, it took a great deal of determination to divert a creek. Charles Camden built the ditch on Crystal Creek between 1855 and 1858, and it was apparently intended to supply water for his house, his orchard, and for streamside placer gold mines. Along with the water from another ditch on Mill Creek, Camden not only had enough water for his purposes, but was able to sell the surplus to other miners. After 150 years, the Crystal Creek Water Ditch is still in use, delivering water to the orchard.

From the cleanout house, the original water ditch continued along the hillside across Crystal Creek Road, where it dropped into a 900-foot U-tube, or siphon, which carried the water down and across the ravine now carrying Highway 299. Constructed of bored-out, 12-foot pine logs, water entered the upstream end of the siphon and emerged at its own level on the other side of the small canyon.

KEY POINTS

0.0 Crystal Creek Water Ditch Trailhead.

0.4 Trestle and boardwalk.

0.8 Headworks on Crystal Creek.

Trinity River

The Trinity River emerges from Lewiston Dam and runs generally west as it cuts a deep canyon through the Klamath Mountains. In recognition of the Trinity River's exceptional qualities, it has been designated a Wild and Scenic River. Long stretches of the river are closely paralleled by Highway 299, which gives boaters, anglers, and other recreational users easy access. This book covers the Trinity River from Lewiston Dam downstream to Burnt Ranch Campground.

Runnable most of the year, the Trinity River is very popular with whitewater rafters and kayakers. Most boaters put in at Pigeon Point and are strongly advised to take out at Cedar Flat or before.

From Pigeon Point to Cedar Flat, the Trinity River is primarily Class II and III whitewater. Downstream from Cedar Flat, the river enters Burnt Ranch Gorge, which is Class V and recommended only for expert boaters.

Several commercial operators offer guided raft trips and whitewater instruction along the Trinity River. Contact the U.S. Forest Service offices in Weaverville or Big Bar for company names and phone numbers (see Appendix A).

Visitor Centers and Amenities

The U.S. Forest Service ranger station in Weaverville, at the junction of Highway 299 and Highway 3, is the main source of information about the Trinity

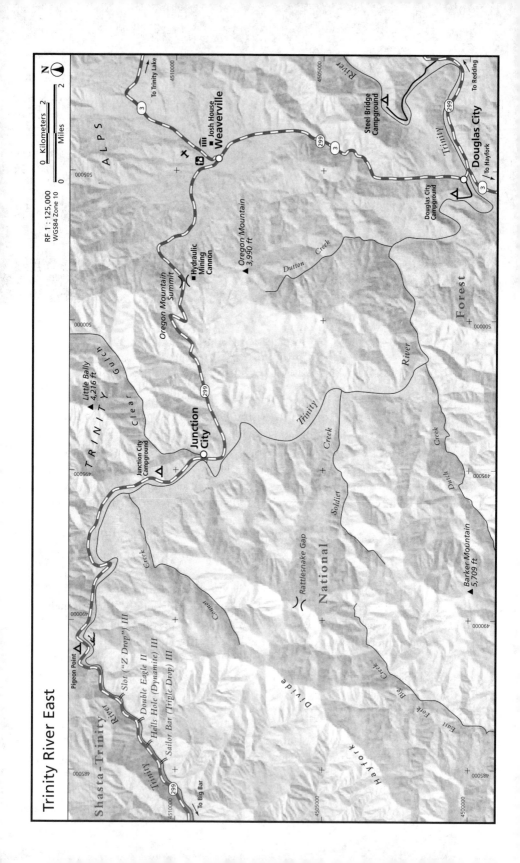

Trinity River East

RF 1 : 125,000
WGS84 Zone 10

N

0   Kilometers   2

0   Miles   2

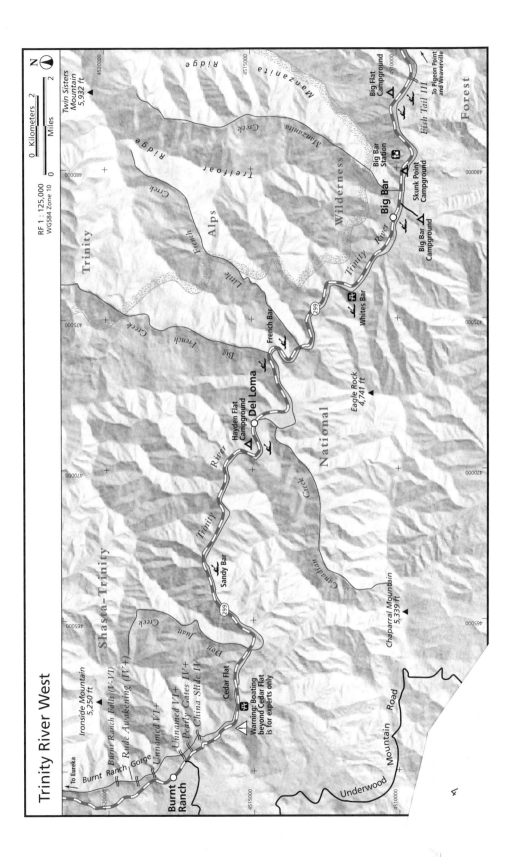

Trinity River West

RF 1 : 125,000
WGS84 Zone 10

N

0 Kilometers 2
0 Miles 2

Trinity   Alps

Twin Sisters Mountain
5,932 ft

Treltoar Ridge

Manzanita Ridge

Manzanita Creek

French Creek

Little French Creek

Big French Creek

French Bar

Whites Bar
299

Wilderness

Big Bar Station

Big Flat Campground

Skunk Point Campground

Big Bar Campground

Big Bar

Trinity River

Fish Tail III

To Pigeon Point
and Weaverville

Forest

National

Eagle Rock
4,741 ft

Hayden Flat Campground

Del Loma

Trinity River

Sandy Bar
299

Chaparral Mountain
5,339 ft

Canadian Creek

Ironside Mountain
5,250 ft

To Eureka

Shasta–Trinity

Burnt Ranch Falls (I–VI)
Rude Awakening (IV+)
Unnamed VI+
Pearly Gates IV+
China Slide IV
Cedar Flat

Burnt Ranch Gorge
Unnamed V+

Burnt Ranch

Don Juan Creek

Warning: Boating
beyond Cedar Flat
is for experts only

Underwood   Mountain   Road

4

River. From Lewiston Dam to just above Pigeon Point, the Trinity River is on Bureau of Land Management (BLM) lands. The town of Weaverville is also the main supply point for the river area.

Campgrounds

This section lists the public campgrounds along the Trinity River from Lewiston to Burnt Ranch. There are numerous private campgrounds along this section of river as well.

The Bureau of Land Management has three campgrounds along its section of the Trinity River. Since Highway 299 does not closely follow the river through most of this section of mixed private and federal land, access to the BLM campgrounds is via side roads from Highway 299.

Steel Bridge Campground is located on the left bank of the Trinity River a few miles downstream of the town of Lewiston. From Douglas City, drive 3 miles east on Highway 299, then turn left onto Steel Bridge Road. Drive 2 miles to the campground. The campground has nine sites, water, and day-use parking.

Douglas City Campground is on the right bank of the Trinity River near Douglas City. From Highway 299 0.5 mile west of Douglas City, turn at Steiner Canyon Road. The campground has water and twenty units, as well as a day-use picnic area.

Junction City Campground is located on the right bank of the Trinity River a couple of miles west of Junction City. This campground has water and twenty-two units and is open all year.

The remainder of the campgrounds along the Trinity River, from Pigeon Point to Burnt Ranch, are in the Shasta–Trinity National Forest. Some of the campgrounds are also river access points.

Pigeon Point Campground is a few miles west of Junction City on Highway 299, on the right bank of the Trinity River. Open all year, this small campground has three units and no water. Pigeon Point is also a river access point and has a beach area.

Big Flat Campground is about 5 miles west of Pigeon Point Campground, on the right bank of the Trinity River. The campground has water and ten units and is open all year.

Skunk Point Group Campground is a couple of miles west of Big Flat, on the right bank of the river. Water is not available. Reservations must be made through Big Bar Station (530–623–6106). The area is closed to camping and open to day use only from December 1 through March 1.

Big Bar Campground is 1 mile west of Skunk Point Campground, on the left bank of the Trinity River, and has three units without water.

Burnt Ranch Falls on the Trinity River.

Whites Bar Picnic Area is about 2 miles west of Skunk Point Campground and is a day-use area on the right bank of the Trinity River. Whites Bar is also a good wildlife viewing area.

Hayden Flat Campground is on the right bank of the river near Canadian Bar. It has water, thirty-six units, is wheelchair-accessible, and is open all year.

Cedar Flat Picnic Area is on the right bank of the Trinity River about 6 miles west of Canadian Bar and is a day-use area, as well as a river access point.

Burnt Ranch Campground is nestled on the steep slopes between Highway 299 and the left bank of the Trinity River. It has sixteen units and water. There is no river access.

Scenic Drives

Highway 299 closely parallels the Trinity River from Junction City to Cedar Flat, and the highway is an exceptionally scenic drive. As the highway winds along the river, it is interesting to watch how the canyon becomes progressively drier as the river descends westward through the mountains. The public campgrounds and picnic areas listed above all offer at least foot access to the river, and there are numerous pullouts where you can enjoy the views.

There are several private campgrounds and resorts along the river, most of which offer access to the river. Because some portions of the highway and river run through private land, please respect all posted private land and do not enter without permission.

Water Access

River access is available at Bagdad, Pigeon Point, Sailor Bar, Big Flat, Big Bar, Whites Bar, French Bar, between French Bar and Cedar Flat, and at Cedar Flat Picnic Area.

Whitewater on the Trinity River is rated according to the standard whitewater classification system, which has six classes:

Class I is novice whitewater, with moving water with a few riffles and small waves, and few or no obstructions.

Class II requires basic boating skills. Expect rapids with waves up to 3 feet, wide, clear channels, but some maneuvering to get past obvious obstacles.

Class III whitewater has rapids with high, irregular waves, narrow channels, and rocks and holes. Complex maneuvering should be expected, and boaters should scout before running.

Class IV is dangerous for swimming. Expect the rapids to be long and turbulent with powerful waves and holes. Numerous obstacles require constant, precise maneuvering. Scouting is mandatory.

Class V is considered the limit of reasonable boating. Expect long, technical, and very violent rapids with highly congested routes. Dangerous drops, unstable eddies, irregular currents, and horrendous holes are often encountered. This class requires experience, confidence, fitness, and proper equipment. Every passage must be scouted.

Class VI is unrunnable for most boaters and is considered nearly impossible and extremely dangerous. Mistakes can be fatal. Only expert teams should attempt Class VI after close and careful study.

It is 25 river miles from Pigeon Point to Cedar Flat. From Pigeon Point to mile 5.2, the Trinity River is rated Class III+. From mile 5.2 to Cedar Flat, the river is rated Class II+. Remember that river levels affect the difficulty of rapids and can fluctuate quickly, depending on water releases from the dams and seasonal runoff. Although the Trinity River can be run year-round, it is best in late spring and summer. Runnable levels range from 500 to 8,000 cubic feet per second; flow information is available at (530) 322–3327. Purify river water before drinking. The shuttle, on Highway 299, is 24 miles.

Rapids on the Trinity River near Big Flat.

Maps: Helena, Hayfork Bally, Big Bar, Del Loma, Ironside Mountain (USGS), Shasta–Trinity National Forest (USFS).

Camping along the Trinity River

Camping along the Trinity River is available at the public campgrounds listed above, as well as at several private campgrounds. Elsewhere, you can camp on national forest land. Minimize your impact by camping in open areas on gravel bars or sandy beaches. Pick a campsite tailored to the size of your group. Small groups should avoid taking campsites that can accommodate large groups.

Campfires are rapidly marring the natural appearance of the Trinity River, with blackened stones, piles of charcoal and ashes, and partially burned trash. If you must have a campfire, keep it small, and use a fire pan if at all possible. Never attempt to burn trash. Many food packages contain aluminum foil, which does not burn and remains for decades to mar campsites. Before leaving your campsite, put your fire out by thoroughly mixing the ashes with water, then feeling for heat with the back of your hand. Scatter the fire ring and bury the cold ashes. A free campfire permit is required and can be obtained from any ranger station.

Sanitation

Sanitation is critical if the quality of the river is to be maintained. All trash should be packed out. Try to use the toilets at the public campgrounds and picnic areas if possible. Otherwise, use a river runner's portable toilet, and dispose of the waste outside the river corridor. River water must be purified before drinking it or using it for cooking. Never wash yourself or dishes in the river or side streams. Use biodegradable soap, and dispose of waste water on the ground well away from open water.

Safety and Courtesy

Courtesy goes a long ways toward making the river a pleasant experience for all. Clear launch areas as soon as possible, and avoid conflicts with swimmers and people who are fishing. Move to the opposite side of the river when possible. Be aware of gold dredgers that may be operating under the river, and do not pass directly over them. Watch for cables that stretch across the river to anchor dredges. Most are 6 feet above the river, but some may be at water level. Report any hazardous cables to the Forest Service. Federal regulations require that motorized boats yield the right of way to nonmotorized boats, but this does not give nonmotorized boats the right to block or interfere with motorized boats.

Hypothermia is a serious hazard for boaters. Cold water, as well as rainy, windy weather, can quickly and dangerously lower your body's core temperature. Keep hydrated on the river by drinking at least 2 quarts of water per day, more in hot weather. You should know the weather and river level forecast before your trip. River levels can change rapidly. Study the maps for the section of river you intend to run, and make sure you know the location of the river access points, campgrounds, and charted rapids. Know and respect your river-running ability and that of your party, and never attempt a section of river beyond your skills and equipment.

Trinity Lake Unit:
Whiskeytown–Shasta–
Trinity National
Recreation Area

This unit encompasses both Lewiston and Trinity Lakes, which are reservoirs formed on the Trinity River. Lewiston Lake is the smallest of the four major reservoirs in the Shasta country, at 7 miles in length and with a 15-mile shoreline. Formed in 1961 by the completion of Lewiston Dam, the reservoir serves to direct water into the 11-mile Clear Creek Tunnel for diversion to Whiskeytown Lake and the power plant. Because Lewiston Lake is always kept full and is relatively small in size, it is popular with paddlers and anglers. The entire lake has a 10 miles per hour speed limit. Excellent bird and wildlife watching are found at marshy areas near the center of the lake. Primary access to Lewiston Lake is from County Road 105, which leaves Highway 3 north of Weaverville and runs along the west side of the lake.

At 19 miles in length with a 245-mile shoreline, Trinity Lake is the second-largest lake in the Shasta region. Trinity Lake started to fill in 1961 with the

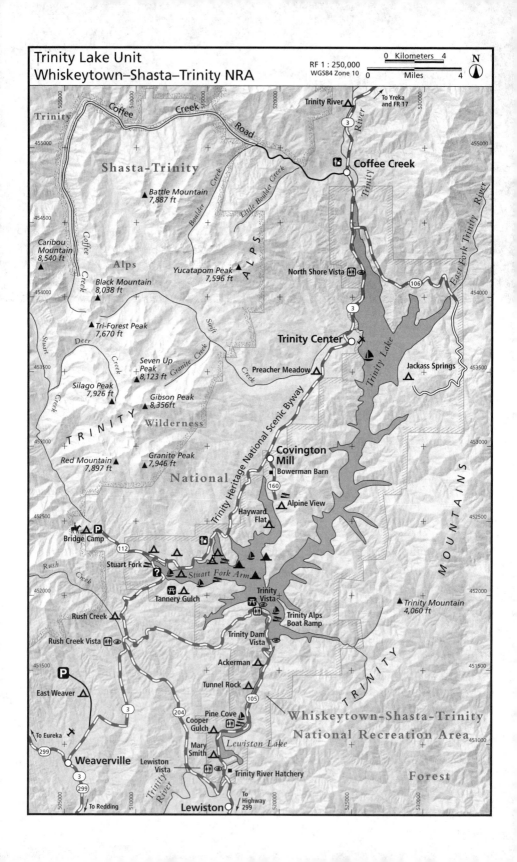

completion of Trinity Dam, and was completely full by 1963. Trinity Dam, 9 miles upstream on the Trinity River from the town of Lewiston, is one of the largest earth-fill dams in the world, running 0.5 mile along the crest and 0.5 mile thick at the base. The dam is 528 feet high. Lake levels vary considerably, as the lake is drawn down to supply water to the northern Central Valley. A building at the base of the dam contains a hydropower facility with enough capacity to power a small city.

Backdropped by the rugged Trinity Alps to the west and the Trinity Mountains to the east, the scenic lake is popular with powerboaters, water-skiers, and anglers. Primary access to Trinity Lake is from Highway 3, along the north and west shores of the Stuart Fork Arm, and the west shore at the north end of the lake. County Road 105 provides access to the south end of the lake, just north of Trinity Dam.

The Stuart Fork Arm, fed by the Stuart and East Forks of the Trinity River, is the most popular area of Trinity Lake. Here you'll find numerous campgrounds, as well as picnic areas, boat ramps, beaches, marinas, and resorts. There is also a lakeside trail.

The long main arm of Trinity Lake, stretching from the dam to the north, has limited road access. Probably the quietest portion of the lake, there are plenty of opportunities to explore secluded, forest-lined coves. There are several boat-in campgrounds, and boaters can camp anywhere along the lakeshore.

From Trinity Center northward, Trinity Lake opens into a broad bay known as the North Lake Area. There are several marinas, and the wide bay is popular with water-skiers.

Visitor Centers and Amenities

The U.S. Forest Service ranger station in Weaverville, at the junction of Highway 299 and Highway 3, is the main source of information for the Trinity Lake Unit. The town of Weaverville is the main point of supply for the Trinity Lake Unit. Supplies are also available at Lewiston, just south of Lewiston Dam on CR 105, and at Trinity Center at the north end of Trinity Lake along Highway 3. There are numerous private resorts and lodges along Highway 3 from Weaverville northward. Pine Cove Marina is located on the west shore of Lewiston Lake, along CR 105. Trinity Alps Marina is on the south end of Trinity Lake and is also reached from CR 105. Estrellita Marina is located on the Stuart Fork Arm, and Trinity Center Marina is on the west shore in the North Lake Area. Both marinas are reached from Highway 3.

Trinity Dam.

Campgrounds

Campgrounds, both drive-in and boat-in, are plentiful in the Trinity Unit. Most of the drive-in campgrounds near the lakes are reached from CR 105 and Highway 3. All of the campgrounds require a fee.

The following campgrounds are along the west shore of Lewiston Lake and are accessible from CR 105.

Mary Smith Campground is located at the south end of Lewiston Lake, along CR 105 just north of Lewiston. It has eighteen tent-only sites and is open May 1 through September 15.

Cooper Gulch Campground is about 2 miles north of Mary Smith Campground, on the west shore of Lewiston Lake, and is reached from CR 105. This small campground is wheelchair-accessible, has five sites, and is open April 1 through October 31.

Tunnel Rock Campground is north of Pine Cove Marina on CR 105. Open all year, this small campground has six sites. There is no water.

Ackerman Campground is near the north end of Lewiston Lake on CR 105. It has sixty-six units and is open all year. Water is available April 1 through October 31.

The largest concentration of campgrounds is located along or near the Stuart Fork Arm of Trinity Lake. These are all accessible from Highway 3.

Rush Creek Campground is just west of Highway 3 along Rush Creek, just north of the Highway 3/CR 105 junction. This ten-unit campground is open May 15 through September 15 and does not have water.

Tannery Gulch Campground is about a mile east of Highway 3 at the end of the Tannery Gulch Road, on the south shore of the Stuart Fork Arm. It is open May 1 through September 30 and has eighty-two sites.

Bridge Camp Campground is west of Trinity Lake along the Stuart Fork of the Trinity River. It is reached by turning west on the Trinity Alps Road (County Road 112) from Highway 3 at the west end of the Stuart Fork Arm of Trinity Lake. The campground is open all year and has water from April 1 through October 31. There are ten sites and horse facilities.

Stoney Point Campground is on the west end of the north shore of the Stuart Fork Arm of Trinity Lake. It has twenty-one units for tents only, is open all year, and has water from May 1 through October 31.

Stoney Point, Fawn, and **Bushytail Group Campgrounds** are all located along the north shore of the Stuart Fork Arm of Trinity Lake. These campgrounds are open from May 1 through September 15 and are available to groups only by advance reservation at (877) 444–6777.

Minersville Campground is located at the end of a spur road east of Highway 3, just south of Mule Creek Forest Service Station. It is open all year, has fourteen sites, and water from May 1 through October 31.

Clark Springs Campground, just north of Minersville Campground, is also reached via a short spur road east of Highway 3. This twenty-one unit campground is open May 1 through October 31 and has water from July 1 through October 31.

Hayward Flat Campground is at the end of Forest Road 35N26Y, east of Highway 3. This large campground has ninety-eight units and is open May 15 through September 15.

Alpine View Campground is along the east shore of the East Fork Stuart Fork Arm of Trinity Lake and is reached via County Road 160 through the settlement of Covington Mill. The fifty-three unit campground is open May 15 through September 15.

Several campgrounds are scattered around the north end of Trinity Lake, but only one, Jackass Springs Campground, is on the lakeshore.

Preacher Meadow Campground is on the west side of Highway 3 about 2 miles south of Trinity Center. It is open from May 15 through October 31 and has forty-five sites.

Goldfield Campground is about 5 miles west of Highway 3 along the Coffee Creek Road (County Road 104). It has six units, no water, and is open all year.

Jackass Springs Campground is on the east shore of Trinity Lake. At the north end of Trinity Lake, leave Highway 3 and drive east and south on County Road 106, then west on County Road 119 to the campground. This twenty-one unit campground is open all year. There is no water and no fee.

Trinity River Campground is north of Trinity Lake, on the Trinity River on the west side of Highway 3. This small campground has seven sites, is open all year, and has water from May 1 through October 31.

Eagle Creek Campground is west of Highway 3 on the Eagle Creek Loop Road. This campground is open May 15 through October 31 and has seventeen sites.

There are four boat-in campgrounds on Trinity Lake: **Captain's Point, Ridgeville, Ridgeville Island, and Mariner's Roost**. Open all year, they vary in size from three to twenty-one units, and have no fee and no water.

Scenic Drives

Trinity Heritage National Scenic Byway

This scenic byway starts from Weaverville and follows Highway 3 north. Then it turns southwest on Rush Creek Road (County Road 204) to Lewiston, where it follows CR 105 north along Lewiston Lake. Turning west along Trinity Lake, the route returns to Highway 3 and follows it north past Trinity Lake. The final portion of the scenic byway follows Parks Creek Road (County Road 17) over the Trinity Divide and ends at Interstate 5 northwest of the town of Mount Shasta. Allow at least a day to enjoy all the attractions and historic sites along the route.

Weaverville's picturesque downtown features historic brick buildings that were mostly built after the devastating fire of 1854. Many western towns have gone through the same cycle of boom construction and fire, where the original wooden buildings were destroyed and replaced with more fire-resistant brick or stone. To get a better feel for the history and heritage of Weaverville, visit the **Joss House** and the **Jake Jackson Museum.** Weaverville reached a population of 10,000 during the gold rush era.

On the way north out of town on Highway 3, watch for a historic marker on the right, which tells the story of the infamous Chinese Tong War of 1854.

About 4 miles north of Weaverville, Highway 3 enters the **Shasta–Trinity National Forest.** Before the merger of the two forests in 1954, the Trinity National Forest had its headquarters in Weaverville, which is still the site of a ranger station. The Shasta–Trinity National Forest is headquartered in Redding, a more central point for the management of the vast area encompassed by the combined forests. Originally created primarily for timber production, grazing, and the protection of wildlife and watersheds, the mission of the Shasta–Trinity National Forest has been expanded to meet the increasing demand for recreation, as well as the management of minerals, water quality, fisheries, and archaeological and historic sites. Keep in mind that there are inholdings of private land within the national forest, where commercial activities such as subdivisions, mining, and logging may take place unregulated by the U.S. Forest Service. Always obtain permission before entering private land, except on public roads or trails.

At the junction of Highway 3 and CR 204, 3 miles north of the forest boundary, you'll turn right onto CR 204, but first, stop at **Rush Creek Vista** to enjoy the view and pick up brochures at the self-serve information station. County Road 204 descends for about 9 miles along Rush Creek through fine meadows and dense mixed conifer forest. Stacks of bare rock along Rush Creek remain from the heavy mining during the gold rush.

At the small town of Lewiston, turn right and cross **Old Lewiston Bridge** and the **Trinity River.** The present steel bridge was built in 1900 to replace earlier log bridges that repeatedly washed away in floods. As with all one-lane bridges, the first vehicle on the bridge has the right-of-way. On the far side of the bridge you'll enter historic Lewiston.

Originally named Lewis Town, after B. F. Lewis, who built a trading post and a ferry on the Trinity River below the present bridge in the 1840s, the settlement became a bustling cultural center during the gold rush. When the miners moved on, the town became a quiet center for farming, ranching, timber production, and leftover mining. Boom times returned in 1957, when construction began on Lewiston and Trinity Dams and workers poured into the area. After the completion of the dams in 1962, Lewiston again went bust. However, the increasing number of people seeking outdoor recreation in the area has since created an economic recovery in Lewiston that is more reliable in the long term than the boom-and-bust cycle of mining.

From Lewiston, drive north on Deadwood Road to the intersection with Trinity Dam Boulevard (CR 105). Cross CR 105 and follow the signs to the **Sven-Olbertson Side Channel.** This interpretive stop is located just before the **Trinity River Fish Hatchery.** Along this stretch of the Trinity River below Lewiston Dam, the U.S. Forest Service and several cooperating partners constructed holding water, nursery areas, and spawning beds for salmon and steelhead. This work also enhanced the streamside vegetation, creating an excellent area for viewing wildlife, including birds.

From the interpretive site, turn left and continue to the Trinity River Fish

Hatchery. Operated by the California Department of Fish and Game, the hatchery is open to the public. Built after the construction of Lewiston Dam, the hatchery is a spawning facility intended to replace the spawning grounds lost with the flooding of the upper Trinity River by the two dams. Touring the hatchery is especially rewarding during the spring and fall steelhead and salmon runs. The section of Trinity River between Lewiston Dam and Old Lewiston Bridge is considered excellent fly fishing and attracts fly-fishing enthusiasts from all over the world.

Above the hatchery looms **Lewiston Dam,** an earth-fill structure. The primary purpose of the dam is to divert water into the Clear Creek Tunnel, which begins underwater on the east side of the dam. The tunnel is 18 feet in diameter and runs for 11 miles under the Trinity Divide to the Judge Francis J. Carr Powerhouse above Whiskeytown Lake. After running through the powerhouse, the water flows into Whiskeytown Lake, where it is diverted south to support the cities and farms in the northern Central Valley.

To continue on the Trinity Heritage National Scenic Byway, retrace your route to CR 105, then turn right. A mile up CR 105, you'll come to **Lewiston Vista,** which offers an overview of the southern end of Lewiston Lake. To keep a constant flow through Clear Creek Tunnel, the lake is kept full, which enhances the reservoir's appearance and makes it popular for fishing and paddling. Although powerboats are allowed on Lewiston Lake, speeds are limited to 10 miles per hour to preserve the quiet. Because the waters of the lake are drawn from the depths of Trinity Lake, the water is cold and provides good habitat for eastern brook, brown, and rainbow trout.

Across from the vista and now submerged by the lake, an area known as "**Starvation Flat**" was the scene of a disaster in the late 1860s. Deep snows and heavy flooding isolated a Chinese mining camp on a bend in the Trinity River, and several miners died as a result.

From Lewiston Vista, turn right, and drive north on CR 105 to **Pine Cove Interpretive Site.** This site features a boat ramp as well as a lakeside picnic area. Because some parts of the shoreline of Lewiston Lake are marshy, it is perfect habitat for ducks, other waterfowl, and migrating songbirds. The observation platform is a good place to watch osprey and bald eagles fishing.

To the west of Pine Cove Interpretive Site, a place known as **Bald Hill,** an area of rich gold deposits, was mined with water brought from Stuart Fork by one of the longest ditches ever constructed to bring water to a gold-mining site. To the north, Pettijohn Mountain is truly a bald summit, the mountain having been stripped of its rock and soil to provide fill material for Trinity Dam.

From Pine Cove, continue north on CR 105 along the scenic west shore of **Lewiston Lake.** Near Tunnel Rock Campground, a man named Mooney operated a ferry across the Trinity River on a pack trail that connected French

Pine Cove on Lewiston Lake.

Gulch and the gold field on the Trinity River. The miners, in turn, were following a route created by the Wintu Indians traveling between winter villages on Clear Creek and summer fishing camps on the Trinity River. Mooney's ferry operated until the first log bridge was built across the river at the present site of Trinity Dam.

Trinity Dam Overlook is the next stop on the scenic drive. About 2 miles north of the dam, stop at **Trinity Vista** for a view of **Trinity Lake** and the surrounding **Trinity Alps** and **Trinity Mountains**. Trinity Lake is popular with houseboaters, anglers, and water-skiers. Numerous forested coves provide quiet places to fish or camp. The Trinity Alps form the skyline to the west and northwest. The 513,000-acre Trinity Alps Wilderness was designated by Congress in

1984. As with other units of the National Wilderness Preservation System, the Trinity Alps Wilderness is managed to preserve its primitive character. Mining, logging, roads, and mechanized equipment are prohibited in the wilderness. A network of trails provides access for hikers and equestrians to the spectacular peaks, alpine meadows, and mountain streams of the wilderness.

The lower slopes of the Trinity Alps, outside the wilderness, as well as the Trinity Mountains to the northeast, are managed for multiple use, including logging. Several of these logging cuts are visible from Trinity Vista.

After leaving Trinity Vista, drive west on CR 105 9 miles to Highway 3, then turn right. The highway crosses Slate Creek Divide and descends to cross the Stuart Fork Arm of Trinity Lake. Continue along the west side of the lake to Guy Covington Drive, which is 9 miles from the CR 105 intersection. Turn right on Guy Covington Drive and head south through the small community of Covington Mill to the next stop on the scenic drive, **Bowerman Barn**.

Bowerman Barn, now on the National Register of Historic Places, is the only building remaining from the old Bowerman Homestead. A rare structure with a foundation of hand-laid cut stone, a mortise-and-tenon framework, and siding of whipsawn pine boards fastened with hand-forged square nails, it too has nearly succumbed to the effects of time and weather. Efforts are under way to restore the barn as near to its original condition as possible.

After returning to Highway 3 on Guy Covington Drive, turn right to continue along the Heritage Tour 6 miles to Trinity Center. Originally called Trinity Centre, the town was settled in 1851 and soon became a trading center for the ranches and mines in the area, as well as an important stop on the Portland–Sacramento Stage Road. The original town site now lies under Trinity Lake, and the new town was built on land donated by the Scott family, owners of the Scott Ranch. Their ranch was one of many ranches and small farms along the upper Trinity River that were drowned by the rising waters of the reservoir, which marked the end of the ranching period and the beginnings of a local economy based on recreation.

During, the gold rush era, a supply trail along Swift Creek linked Trinity Center with Abram's Trading Post at Big Flat. Mules and horses were used to carry supplies that were ultimately destined for the mines above Coffee Creek. The trail is now one of the most popular routes in the Trinity Alps.

Several historic buildings were moved to the new Trinity Center town site and preserve a link to the town's past, including the **International Order of Odd Fellows Hall**. Another site worth visiting is the **Scott Museum**, which features a large collection of historic objects from the area.

Continue the tour by driving north along Highway 3 to **North Shore Vista.**

Under Trinity Lake in front of the North Shore Vista is the site of **Stringtown**, a small settlement that grew up along the old stage road, on the site of

Bowerman Barn on the Trinity Heritage National Scenic Byway.

the Graves Ranch. When lake levels drop in the fall, tailing piles from the mining era sometimes become visible. These are the products of dredge mining, which used giant floating mechanized dredges to rip up the soil, sand, and gravel of the riverbed to extract minute traces of gold. The tailings are a visible reminder of the period in which mining dominated the economy and the politics of the area.

From North Shore Vista, turn right on Highway 3 and head 3 miles north past the north end of Trinity Lake to Carrville Road, and turn left. This short loop road takes you to **Carrville Inn**.

The historic Carrville Inn was built in the late 1800s to serve travelers on the Portland–Sacramento Stage Road. Now renovated and open as a bed-and-breakfast, the inn has changed little in over one hundred years. During the gold-mining period, Carrville was a busy town with a general store, hotel, and other facilities. It is claimed that future president Herbert Hoover stayed in Carrville while working as a mining engineer in the area. Carrville was also a major social center when winter closed down the mines.

Prior to the construction of the railroad up the Sacramento River Valley north of Redding, the Portland–Sacramento Stage Road was the main north-south artery connecting the major cities of Oregon and northern California. Developed at the beginning of the gold rush from trails pioneered by Native Americans and European explorers, the route was established as a pack trail. Private capital was used to construct a road passable to wagons and stages, which was operated as a toll road. The stage road saw a steadily increasing stream of wagons, mule trains, and automobiles. It remained a dirt road, hot and dusty during the summer and deep with mud and snow in the winter, when it was often impassable for weeks at a time. The last stage traveled the road in 1924. Highway 3 became the first paved highway when the road was moved to its present route along the west side of Trinity Lake during the construction of the dam. Carrville Road is one the few surviving sections of the old stage road. Other sections include Highway 3 from Sunflower Flat to Callahan, and the Bear Creek and Eagle Creek loops.

During the summer of 1958, while Highway 3 was being rerouted, sparks from heavy machinery started a forest fire that soon crossed the Trinity River and roared up the slopes of the Trinity Mountains. Workers from the Trinity Dam site were diverted to fight the fire, causing construction of the dam to almost stop until the fire was controlled. More than fifty years later, scars from the fire are still visible in the form of clearings regrown with low brush, along with small trees grown up from plantings made after the fire.

From the Carrville Inn, follow Carrville Road north to Highway 3, then turn left. Coffee Creek, the next stop on the scenic byway, is just 0.25 mile north.

Coffee Creek is a small community located just north of the national recreation area in the upper Trinity Valley. Now the jumping-off point for trips into the Trinity Alps, Coffee Creek was once the center for a cluster of gold mines that rivaled the gold strikes in the famous Klondike country in Alaska and Canada. Thousands of mines, large and small, were established along Coffee Creek and the Trinity River, and their remains can be seen in the area today.

Coffee Creek may have received its name from an accident in which a pack train loaded with coffee for the mines got caught in a flash flood and washed away. More likely, the name came from the coffee color of the creek during winter and spring runoff. Coffee Creek is your last chance to refuel and resupply before the end of the scenic drive 39 miles northeast on Interstate 5.

From Coffee Creek, continue north on Highway 3. This very pretty section of highway crosses the Trinity River several times as it winds through the heavily forested headwaters of the river. Fishing and camping are both very popular along the upper Trinity.

Ten miles north of Coffee Creek, turn right on the International Paper Road (CR 17), also known as the Parks Creek Road. Although this road is paved, it is steep and winding in places, and drivers should use extra care. From the junction, continue 5 miles to the next stop at the **modern gold mine.** This site is an example of how modern mining methods and equipment can reach ore that was too difficult during the gold rush era. From the mine site, continue on CR 17 6 miles to the next stop, the Sisson–Callahan National Recreation Trail.

This trail was established by trappers, prospectors, and ranchers in the mid-1800s by linking trails followed by the natives, and connected the Mount Shasta area with the upper Trinity River area. The U.S. Forest Service improved the trail in the early twentieth century, shortly after the creation of the Shasta National Forest, and used it for access to patrol areas within this portion of the forest. The west end of the Sisson–Callahan National Recreation Trail is on CR 17 just west of the Parks Creek Divide, and the east end is along CR 17 above Lake Siskiyou.

Three miles farther along, CR 17 crosses **Parks Creek Divide,** the highest point of the road. Here, on this windswept ridge of alpine meadows and trees, the **Pacific Crest Trail** crosses the paved road. This national scenic trail runs 2,600 miles from Canada to Mexico and is one of the most popular long trails in the country. Through-hikers attempt to hike the entire trail in one season, but even more popular is day hiking, backpacking, or horseback riding along a portion of this spectacular, high-altitude trail. A good, easy hike runs from Parks Creek Divide 3 miles south to **Deadfall Lakes.**

Visible to the east of Parks Creek Divide, **Mount Eddy** is the highest point in Trinity County, at 9,025 feet, and sits directly across the Shasta Valley from Mount Shasta. Several fire lookout structures have been built on its summit,

A snag along Pacific Crest National Scenic Trail.

and a good trail leads from the Pacific Crest Trail to the top of the mountain. A hike to the top is rewarded by a panoramic, 360-degree view of Mount Shasta, the Shasta Valley, the Trinity Divide, and the Trinity Alps. Lakes and springs around Mount Eddy form the sources of the Sacramento, Trinity, and Shasta Rivers.

Mount Shasta dominates the view to the northeast, towering 14,162 feet. A landmark visible for miles in all directions, Mount Shasta is the centerpiece of the Shasta region.

From Parks Creek Divide, CR 17 and the Trinity Heritage National Scenic Byway continue 12 miles to end at I–5. Along the way, you'll get several good views of Mount Shasta as the road descends into the Shasta Valley. Or, if desired, you can turn around at Parks Creek Divide and retrace CR 17 and Highway 3 to Weaverville.

Fishing

The length of the Trinity River downstream of Lewiston Dam is known as the "Fly Stretch," and it offers world-class fly fishing.

Lewiston Lake, since it is cold and held at a constant level, is an excellent trout fishery. Brown and brook trout are common, and rainbow trout are abundant. Several campgrounds located along CR 105 on the west shore offer access to the lake. The main boat ramp is located at Pine Cove. Lewiston Lake has a 10 miles per hour speed limit.

Trinity Lake has been designated a "Trophy Black Bass" lake by the California Department of Fish and Game, and the state record smallmouth bass and brown bullhead were caught here. The mouths of large tributaries are good places to fish for trout in the spring and summer. Species include smallmouth and largemouth bass, chinook, catfish, kokanee, and rainbow and brown trout. Numerous campgrounds and picnic areas offer access to the lake along its west shore, and there are several boat ramps and marinas.

The California Department of Fish and Game regulates fishing, and a valid fishing license is required.

Water Sports

Lewiston Lake, being smaller and at a constant level, is a good lake for canoeists, kayakers, and other paddlers. Although powerboats are allowed, there is a 10 miles per hour speed limit on the entire lake. Portions of the shoreline are marshy, which provides good waterfowl and wildlife viewing opportunities. Primary boat access is the Pine Cove Boat Ramp, located on the west shore of the lake off CR 105.

Boating on Lewiston Lake.

Trinity Lake, because of its size, is popular with powerboaters, although paddlers who enjoy longer paddles may also enjoy it, especially during the off-season. There are several boat ramps and marinas along the west shore. Fairview Boat Ramp and Trinity Alps Marina are at the south end of the lake, between the dam and Trinity Vista off CR 105. Stuart Fork Boat Ramp is located at the west end of Stuart Fork, off Highway 3. Cedar Stock Boat Ramp and Marina is located on the north shore of Stuart Fork, off Highway 3. Minersville Boat Ramp is located at Minersville Campground, west of Highway 3. Bowerman Boat Ramp is just north of Alpine View Campground. Boat ramps are also located at Clark Springs Campground, Estrellita Marina, Trinity Center Marina, and Wyntoon Resort. Some boat ramps become unusable as Trinity Lake is drawn down, and others can be clogged with floating debris. There is a fee for the use of most boat ramps.

There are two swim beaches on Trinity Lake. One is located at Stoney Creek Group Campground and the other at Clark Springs Campground.

Trails

Hiking and single-track mountain biking is limited near Lewiston and Trinity Lakes. There are nature trails at Alpine View and Tannery Gulch Campgrounds, and there are several lakeshore trails along Lewiston and Trinity Lakes. The nearby Trinity Alps offer many miles of wilderness trails for hikers and backpackers (see the Trinity Alps chapter).

South Lakeshore Trail

See map on page 70.

HIGHLIGHTS: A scenic trail along the west shore of Lewiston Lake.

TYPE OF TRIP: Out-and-back.

DISTANCE: 1.4 miles.

DIFFICULTY: Easy.

PERMITTED USES: Hiking, horses, mountain bikes.

MAPS: Whiskeytown–Shasta–Trinity National Recreation Area Topographic Map (Earthwalk Press), Lewiston (USGS).

SPECIAL CONSIDERATIONS: None.

PARKING AND FACILITIES: The south trailhead is north of Mary Smith Campground off CR 105, and the north trailhead is located at Cooper Gulch Campground.

FINDING THE TRAILHEAD: From Lewiston, drive north on CR 105 to Mary Smith Campground. Continue north on CR 105 0.5 mile, then turn right to the South Shore Trailhead.

Starting from the south trailhead, this easy trail follows the west shore of Lewiston Lake through old-growth Douglas fir. The trail ends at Cooper Gulch Campground.

North Lakeshore Trail

HIGHLIGHTS: A scenic trail along the west side of Lewiston Lake with opportunities for wildlife viewing.

TYPE OF TRIP: Out-and-back.

DISTANCE: 4 miles.

DIFFICULTY: Easy.

PERMITTED USES: Hiking, horses, mountain biking.

MAPS: Whiskeytown–Shasta–Trinity National Recreation Area Topographic Map (Earthwalk Press), Trinity Dam (USGS).

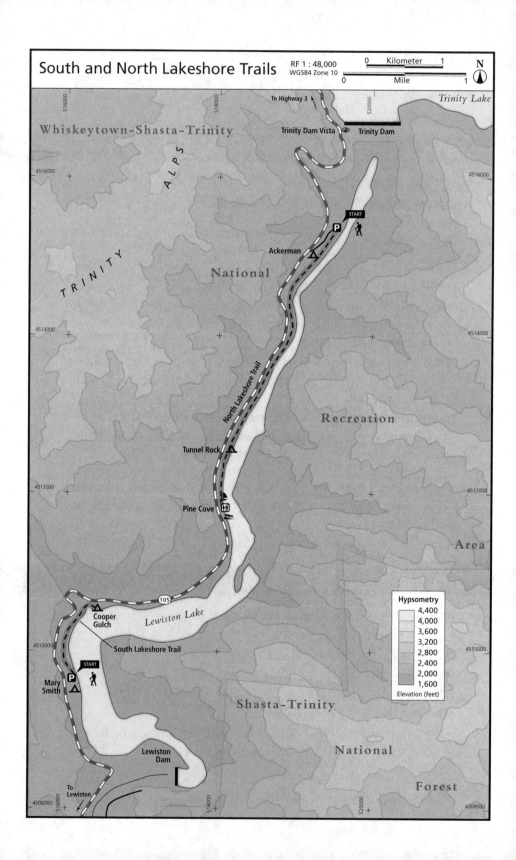

SPECIAL CONSIDERATIONS: There is no shade, so bring plenty of water and a hat during the summer.

PARKING AND FACILITIES: The trailhead is located at Ackerman Campground.

FINDING THE TRAILHEAD: From Lewiston, drive north on County Road 105 to Ackerman Campground, on the right, and park at the signed trailhead.

Starting from the trailhead at Ackerman Campground, this trail takes you along the west shore of Lewiston Lake. It passes by Tunnel Rock Campground and ends at Pine Cove. There is no shade along the trail, so wear a sunhat and bring plenty of water during the summer.

KEY POINTS

0.0 Trailhead at Ackerman Campground.

1.3 Tunnel Rock Campground.

2.0 Pine Cove Boat Ramp and Picnic Area.

Trinity Lakeshore Trail

HIGHLIGHTS: A nearly level lakeshore trail connecting Clark Springs Campground and Pinewood Cove Resort.

TYPE OF TRIP: Out-and-back.

DISTANCE: 7.2 miles.

DIFFICULTY: Moderate.

PERMITTED USES: Hiking, mountain biking.

MAPS: Whiskeytown–Shasta–Trinity National Recreation Area Topographic Map (Earthwalk Press), Trinity Dam (USGS).

SPECIAL CONSIDERATIONS: Please stay on the trail when passing through the private resorts.

PARKING AND FACILITIES: Trail users not staying in one of the campgrounds should start from Clark Springs Campground.

FINDING THE TRAILHEAD: From Highway 3 along the west short of Trinity Lake, turn right on the signed turnoff for Clark Springs Campground. Park in the signed trailhead parking area.

The trail stays just above the maximum lake level as it winds though the forest along the lakeshore. At first following the west shore of the small bay at the

Trinity Lakeshore Trail

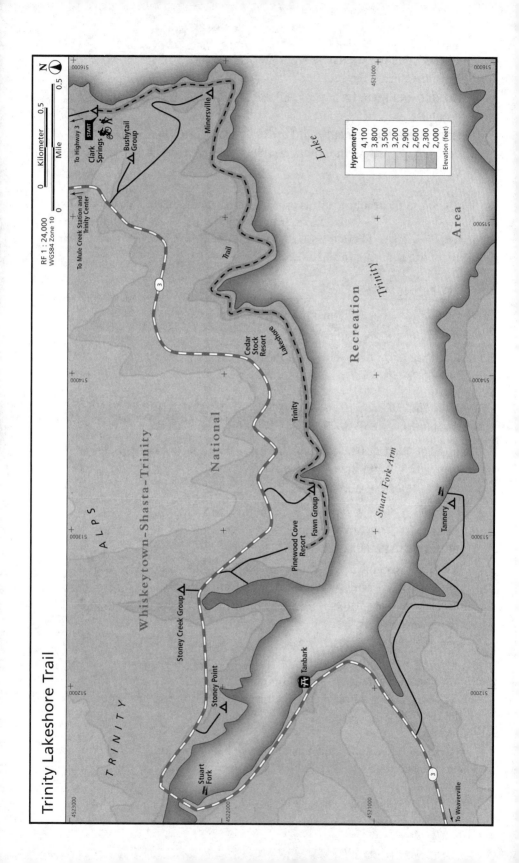

Trinity Lakeshore Trail.

mouth of Mule Creek, the trail soon rounds a point, passing Minersville Camp-ground, and heads west along the north shore of the Stuart Fork Arm. After passing Cedar Stock Resort, the trail continues west past Fawn Group Camp-ground to end at Pinewood Cove.

KEY POINTS

0.0 Clark Springs Trailhead.

0.7 Minersville Campground.

2.1 Cedar Stock Resort.

3.1 Fawn Group Campground.

3.6 Pinewood Cove.

Trinity Alps

The rugged western skyline as seen from the Trinity Lake area is formed by the Trinity Alps. A wild region of rugged, rocky peaks and alpine ridges, these mountains also feature deep, forested glacial canyons, expansive meadows, and alpine lakes. A large portion of the Trinity Alps was protected in 1932 as a U.S. Forest Service Primitive Area, an administrative designation that was intended to preserve the wilderness character of the area. Congress added the Trinity Alps to the National Wilderness Preservation System in 1984, and currently the Trinity Alps Wilderness is 545,000 acres in size, making it one of the largest wilderness areas in California. Although the Trinity Alps span parts of three national forests—the Shasta–Trinity, Six Rivers, and Klamath—only the portion on the Shasta–Trinity National Forest is described in this book.

In wilderness areas, mechanized equipment and travel by mechanized means, including bicycles, are prohibited in order to provide a primitive back-country experience and to protect the area's wild character. An extensive network of trails covers the wilderness, but remember that trail conditions can change. Contact the U.S. Forest Service before your trip to determine the current trail conditions. Access to the wilderness trail system is possible from several trailheads, which are generally reachable via gravel side roads leaving Highway 299 and Highway 3.

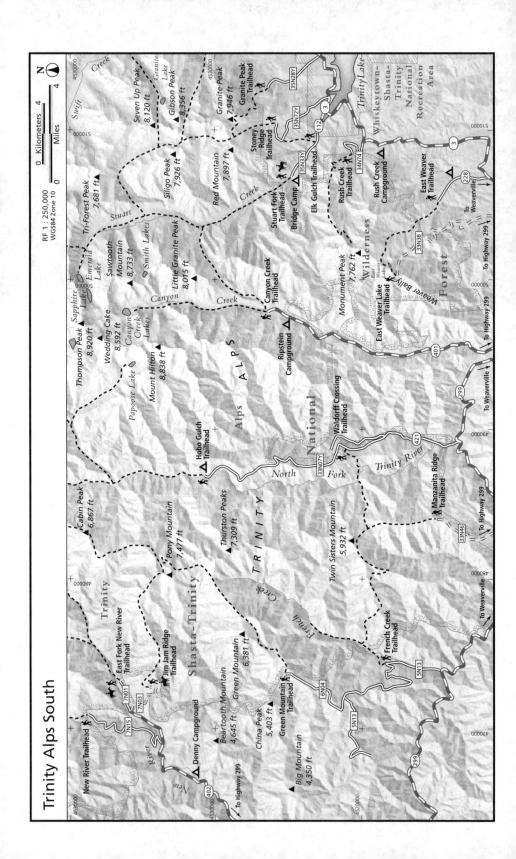

Trinity Alps South

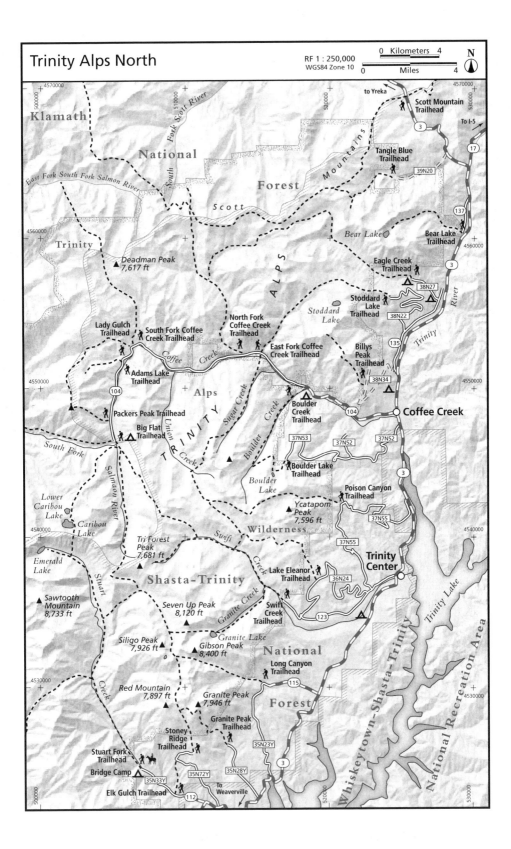

Trinity Alps North

RF 1 : 250,000
WGS84 Zone 10

0 Kilometers 4

0 Miles 4

N

Klamath

National

Forest

Scott

Trinity

Deadman Peak
7,617 ft

ALPS

Scott Mountain
Trailhead

to Yreka

To I-5

3

17

Tangle Blue
Trailhead

39N20

137

Bear Lake

Bear Lake
Trailhead

Eagle Creek
Trailhead

3

38N27

East Fork South Fork Salmon River

South

Fork Scott River

Mountains

Stoddard
Lake

Stoddard
Lake
Trailhead

38N22

Billys
Peak
Trailhead

135

Trinity

River

Lady Gulch
Trailhead

North Fork
Coffee Creek
Trailhead

South Fork Coffee
Creek Trailhead

Coffee

Creek

East Fork Coffee
Creek Trailhead

Adams Lake
Trailhead

104

Alps

Packers Peak Trailhead

Big Flat
Trailhead

South Fork

Salmon River

Union

Creek

Sugar

Creek

TRINITY

Boulder

Creek

Boulder
Creek
Trailhead

104

38N34

Coffee Creek

37N53

37N52

37N52

3

Boulder Lake
Trailhead

Boulder
Lake

Lower
Caribou
Lake

Caribou
Lake

Stuart

Fork

Salmon River

Swift

Creek

Ycatapom
Peak
7,596 ft

Wilderness

Poison Canyon
Trailhead

37N55

37N55

Emerald
Lake

Tri Forest
Peak
7,681 ft

Shasta-Trinity

Lake Eleanor
Trailhead

36N24

Trinity
Center

Trinity Lake

Sawtooth
Mountain
8,733 ft

Seven Up Peak
8,120 ft

Granite

Creek

Swift
Creek
Trailhead

123

Whiskeytown-Shasta-Trinity

Siligo Peak
7,926 ft

Granite Lake

Gibson Peak
8,400 ft

National

Long Canyon
Trailhead

115

National

Recreation

Area

Red Mountain
7,897 ft

Granite Peak
7,946 ft

Forest

Stoney
Ridge
Trailhead

Granite Peak
Trailhead

35N23Y

Stuart Fork
Trailhead

Bridge Camp

35N33Y

35N72Y

35N28Y

3

Elk Gulch Trailhead

112

To
Weaverville

Trinity Alps.

A wilderness permit is required for all overnight or longer entry into the Trinity Alps Wilderness (permits are not required for day use). Permits are available at ranger stations and at self-service stations at trailheads. Group size is strictly limited to ten persons, and the stay limit in the wilderness is fourteen days.

Visitor Centers and Amenities

The U.S. Forest Service ranger station in Weaverville, at the junction of Highway 299 and Highway 3, is the main source of information for the east and south sides of the Trinity Alps, and the town of Weaverville is the main point of supply. Supplies are also available at Lewiston, just south of Lewiston Dam on County Road 105, and at Trinity Center at the north end of Trinity Lake along Highway 3. There are numerous private resorts and lodges along Highway 3 from Weaverville northward, and west of Weaverville on Highway 299 along the Trinity River.

Campgrounds

There are several campgrounds located at trailheads on the south and east sides of the Trinity Alps, or on trailhead access roads. These campgrounds are described in this section. Refer to the Finding the Trailheads section for road directions to these campgrounds. For additional campgrounds in the area, see the Trinity River and Trinity Unit: Whiskeytown–Shasta–Trinity National Recreation Area chapters.

Denny Campground is located on CR 402, the road to Jim Jam, East Fork New River, and New River Trailhead. It has five units, no water, and no fee.

Hobo Gulch Campground is located at the Hobo Gulch Trailhead. It has ten units, no water, and no fee.

Ripstein Campground is on CR 401 near Canyon Creek Trailhead. It has ten units, no water, and no fee.

East Weaver Campground is on CR 228, the access road to East Weaver Lake Trailhead. It has eleven units, with water from April 1 through October 21.

Bridge Camp Campground is at Stuart Fork Trailhead. It has ten units, with water from April 1 through October 21.

Goldfield Campground is near Boulder Creek Trailhead and has six units, no water, and no fee.

Big Flat Campground is located at Big Flat Trailhead. It has five units, no water, and no fee.

Horse Flat Campground is located at the Eagle Creek Trailhead. It has sixteen units, no water, and no fee.

Finding the Trailheads

The following group of trailheads access the south side of the Trinity Alps, via Highway 299 west of Weaverville.

East Weaver Lake Trailhead provides access to the south end of the East Weaver Lake Trail. From Weaverville at the junction of Highway 3 and Highway 299, drive 0.2 mile west on Highway 299, then turn right (north) on Forest Road 33N38. Drive 8.6 miles to the trailhead.

Canyon Creek Trailhead provides access to the south end of the Canyon Creek and Bear Creek Trails. From Weaverville, drive 8.4 miles west on Highway 299 to Junction City. Turn right (north) on CR 401 and drive 12.6 miles to the end of the road. Ripstein Campground is a mile south of the trailhead.

Waldorff Crossing Trailhead provides access to the east end of the Waldorff Crossing Trail. From Weaverville, drive 14.5 miles west on Highway 299, then turn right (north) on CR 421, which is gravel. Drive 6.2 miles to the trailhead.

Hobo Gulch Trailhead gives access to the north end of the Backbone Ridge Trail and the south end of the North Fork Trail. From Weaverville, drive 14.5 miles west on Highway 299, then turn right (north) on CR 421, which is gravel. Drive 15.1 miles to the trailhead at the end of the road.

Manzanita Ridge Trailhead provides access to the south end of the Manzanita Ridge Trail. From Weaverville, drive 20.1 miles west on Highway 299 to Big Flat, then turn right (north) on FR 33N46, an unmaintained road. Drive 2.6 miles to the end of the road.

French Creek Trailhead provides access to the south end of the French Creek Trail. From Weaverville, drive 28.3 miles west on Highway 299, then turn right (north) on FR 5N13. Drive 2.7 miles to the trailhead.

Green Mountain Trailhead accesses the southwest end of the Green Mountain Trail. From Weaverville, drive 28.3 miles west on Highway 299, then turn right (north) on FR 5N13. Drive 8.7 miles, then turn right onto FR 6N04. Drive 3.1 miles, then turn right on FR 6N19. Drive 0.8 mile to the trailhead.

Jim Jam Ridge Trailhead provides access to the Jim Jam Ridge Trail. From Weaverville, drive 45.5 miles west on Highway 299 to Hawkins Bar Picnic Area, then turn right on CR 402. Drive 21.6 miles, passing Denny Campground, and turn right on FR 7N03, an unmaintained road. Drive 2.8 miles to the end of the road.

East Fork New River Trailhead gives access to the south end of the East Fork New River Trail and has horse facilities. From Weaverville, drive 45.5 miles west on Highway 299 to Hawkins Bar Picnic Area, then turn right on CR 402. Drive 23.2 miles, passing Denny Campground, to the end of the road.

New River Trailhead provides access to the south end of the New River Trail and has horse facilities. From Weaverville, drive 45.5 miles west on Highway 299 to Hawkins Bar Picnic Area, then turn right on CR 402. Drive 19.6 miles, passing Denny Campground, then turn left on FR 3N15, a dirt road. Continue 5.7 miles to the end of the road.

The following group of trailheads provides access to the east side of the Trinity Alps from Highway 3 north of Weaverville.

East Weaver Trailhead provides access to the southeast end of the East Weaver Creek Trail and to the northwest end of the Weaver Basin Trail. From Weaverville, drive 1.8 miles north on Highway 3, then turn left (north) on CR 228. Drive 2.6 miles to the end of the road.

Rush Creek Trailhead provides access to the east end of the Rush Creek Lakes Trail. From Weaverville, drive 9.7 miles north on Highway 3, and turn left (west) on FR 34N74. Drive 2.2 miles to the trailhead.

Elk Gulch Trailhead provides access to the south end of the Elk Gulch Trail. From Weaverville, drive 12.9 miles north on Highway 3, and turn left (west) on CR 112, a gravel road. Drive 1.9 miles to the trailhead.

Stuart Fork Trailhead gives access to the southeast end of the Stuart Fork Trail. Bridge Camp Campground and horse facilities are located at the trailhead. From Weaverville, drive 12.9 miles north on Highway 3, then turn left (west) on CR 112, a gravel road. Drive 4.1 miles to the end of the road.

Stoney Ridge Trailhead provides access to the south end of the Stoney Ridge Trail. From Weaverville, drive 13.6 miles north on Highway 3, and then turn left (north) on FR 35N72Y, a gravel road. Drive 4.3 miles to the trailhead.

Granite Peak Trailhead accesses the southeast end of the Granite Peak Trail. From Weaverville, drive 16 miles north on Highway 3, and turn left on FR 35N28Y, a gravel road. This turnoff is opposite the turnoff to Minersville Campground. Drive 2.8 miles to the end of the road.

Long Canyon Trailhead provides access to the east end of the Long Canyon Trail. From Weaverville, drive 22.3 miles north on Highway 3, then turn left (west) on CR 115, a dirt road. Drive 2.6 miles to the trailhead.

The following trailheads are reached from Highway 3 at Trinity Center and northward.

Swift Creek Trailhead accesses the east end of the Swift Creek Trail. From Trinity Center, drive 6.5 miles west on CR 123, a gravel road, to the end of the road.

Lake Eleanor Trailhead provides access to Lake Eleanor and the east end of the Deer Flat Trail. From Trinity Center, drive 1.4 miles west on CR 123, a gravel road, then right (north) on FR 36N24. Drive 6 miles to the trailhead.

Poison Canyon Trailhead accesses the east end of the Poison Canyon Trail. From Trinity Center, drive 1.4 miles west on CR 123, a gravel road, and then right (north) on FR 36N24. Drive 0.4 mile, and turn right (north) on FR 37N55. Drive 5 miles to the trailhead.

Boulder Lake Trailhead provides access to the Boulder Lake Trail. From Trinity Center, drive 7.1 miles north on Highway 3, then left (west) on FR 37N52, a gravel road. Numerous logging roads branch off this road; stay on the main road (which becomes 37N53) 9.2 miles until its end.

The following trailheads are reached from CR 104, a paved and gravel road running west up Coffee Creek from the town of Coffee Creek at Highway 3.

Boulder Creek Trailhead accesses the north end of the Boulder Creek Trail. Goldfield Campground is nearby. From Coffee Creek, drive 4.7 miles west on CR 104, and turn left on FR 37N19Y. Drive 0.6 mile to the trailhead.

East Fork Coffee Creek Trailhead provides access to the south end of the East Fork Coffee Creek Trail. From Coffee Creek, drive 7.4 miles west on CR 104 to the trailhead.

North Fork Coffee Creek Trailhead provides access to the south end of the North Fork Coffee Creek Trail. From Coffee Creek, drive 7.9 miles west on CR 104 to the trailhead.

South Fork Coffee Creek Trailhead accesses the south end of the South Fork Coffee Creek Trail. From Coffee Creek, drive 13.9 miles west on CR 104 to the trailhead.

Lady Gulch Trailhead accesses the east end of the Lady Gulch Trail. From Coffee Creek, drive 14 miles west on CR 104 to the trailhead, which is just 0.1 mile west of South Fork Coffee Creek Trailhead.

Adams Lake Trailhead accesses the east end of the Adams Lake Trail. From Coffee Creek, drive 14.7 miles west on CR 104 to the trailhead.

Packers Peak Trailhead accesses the east end of the Packers Peak Trail. From Coffee Creek, drive 17.3 miles west and south on CR 104 to the trailhead.

Big Flat Trailhead accesses the South Fork Salmon, Caribou Gulch, Caribou Lakes, Tri Forest, and Yellow Rose Trails. Big Flat Campground is located at the trailhead. From Coffee Creek, drive 18.6 miles west and south on CR 104 to the trailhead.

The following trailheads are accessed from Highway 3 between the town of Coffee Creek and Scotts Pass.

Billys Peak Trailhead accesses the south end of the Billys Peak Trail. From the town of Coffee Creek, drive 1.8 miles north on Highway 3, then turn left (west) on FR 38N34, an unmaintained road. This turnoff is just north of Trinity River Campground. Drive 3 miles to the trailhead.

Stoddard Lake Trailhead can be used to access the east end of the Stoddard Lake Trail. From the town of Coffee Creek, drive 2.4 miles north on Highway 3, and turn left (west) on CR 135, the Eagle Creek Loop, which is a gravel road. Drive 1.2 miles, then turn left (west) on FR 38N22. Drive 5.2 miles to the trailhead.

Eagle Creek Trailhead accesses the east end of the Eagle Creek Trail and Horse Flat Campground. From the town of Coffee Creek, drive 2.4 miles north on Highway 3, then turn left (west) on CR 135, the Eagle Creek Loop, which is a gravel road. Drive 2.2 miles, and turn left (west) on FR 38N27, a gravel road. Drive 1 mile to the end of the road.

Bear Lake Trailhead provides access to the east end of the Bear Lake Trail. From the town of Coffee Creek, drive 10.2 miles north on Highway 3, and turn left on CR 137, a gravel road. Drive north 0.8 mile to the trailhead.

Tangle Blue Trailhead accesses the east end of the Grand National Trail. From the town of Coffee Creek, drive 12.7 miles north on Highway 3, and turn left (west) on FR 39N20, an unmaintained dirt road. Drive 2.6 miles to the end of the road.

Scott Mountain Trailhead is an access point on the Pacific Crest National Scenic Trail where it crosses Scotts Pass on Highway 3. This trailhead is 16.7 miles north of the town of Coffee Creek.

Additional trailheads can be used to access the north and west sides of the Trinity Alps in the Klamath and Six Rivers National Forests, which is outside the scope of this book. Consult the Trinity Alps Wilderness USFS map for routes to these trailheads.

Trails

Canyon Creek Lakes

HIGHLIGHTS: A long day hike or multiday backpack trip up a scenic glacial canyon to a pair of alpine lakes.

TYPE OF TRIP: Out-and-back.

DISTANCE: 15.2 miles.

DIFFICULTY: Difficult.

PERMITTED USES: Hiking, horses.

MAPS: Trinity Alps Wilderness (USFS), Mount Hilton (USGS).

SPECIAL CONSIDERATIONS: None.

PARKING AND FACILITIES: Ripstein Campground is located just south of the trailhead.

FINDING THE TRAILHEAD: From Weaverville, drive 8.4 miles west on Highway 299 to Junction City. Turn right (north) on County Road 401, which is a gravel road, and drive 12.6 miles to the end of the road.

Start out on the Canyon Creek Trail, which heads north up Canyon Creek (the Bear Creek Trail leaves the trailhead to the northeast, climbing out of the canyon). Staying on the east slopes just above the creek, the Canyon Creek Trail climbs steadily up the forested canyon.

Just before the trail reaches Canyon Creek Falls, it climbs more steeply past an area known as "The Sinks," where the main creek and several tributaries disappear underground for a short distance before reappearing farther down canyon. Canyon Creek Falls is a few yards west of the trail.

The ascent moderates as the trail enters Upper Canyon Creek Meadows. Just above another short ascent, the Boulder Creek Lakes Trail comes in on the left. The Canyon Creek Trail continues north up Canyon Creek and climbs steeply to lower Canyon Creek Lake. The trail now skirts this lake on the west to reach a point between the lower and upper lakes. This scenic point is the end of the hike.

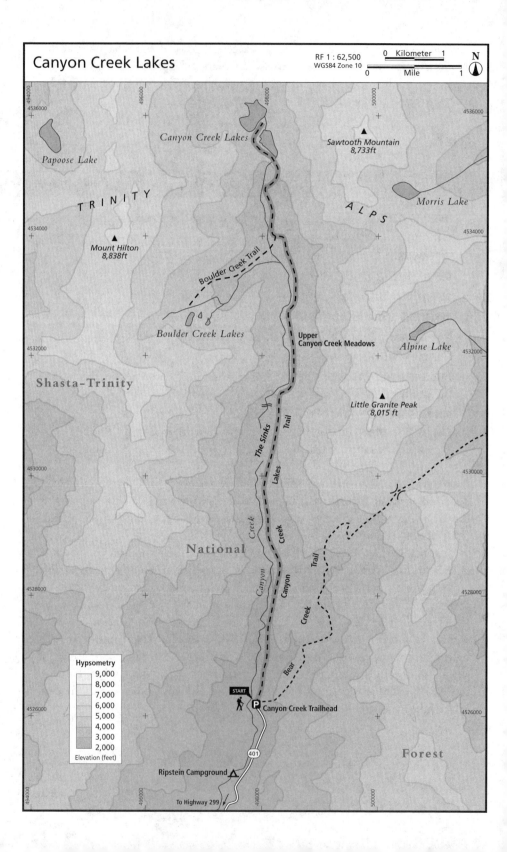

Canyon Creek Lakes

RF 1 : 62,500
WGS84 Zone 10

0 Kilometer 1

0 Mile 1

N

Papoose Lake

Canyon Creek Lakes

Sawtooth Mountain
8,733ft

T R I N I T Y

A L P S

Morris Lake

Mount Hilton
8,838ft

Boulder Creek Trail

Boulder Creek Lakes

Upper
Canyon Creek Meadows

Alpine Lake

Shasta–Trinity

Little Granite Peak
8,015 ft

The Sinks

Lakes Trail

National

Canyon Creek

Canyon Creek Trail

Bear Creek

Hypsometry

9,000
8,000
7,000
6,000
5,000
4,000
3,000
2,000

Elevation (feet)

START

P Canyon Creek Trailhead

401

Forest

Ripstein Campground △

To Highway 299

KEY POINTS

0.0 Canyon Creek Trailhead.

3.1 The Sinks.

3.6 Canyon Creek Falls.

4.4 Upper Canyon Creek Meadows.

5.5 Trail to Boulder Creek Lakes on left; continue on Canyon Creek Trail.

6.3 Lower lake.

7.6 Canyon Creek Lakes.

Emerald Lake

HIGHLIGHTS: A multiday backpack trip to an alpine lake set under Sawtooth Ridge.

TYPE OF TRIP: Out-and-back.

DISTANCE: 22.2 miles.

DIFFICULTY: Difficult.

PERMITTED USES: Hiking, horses.

MAPS: Trinity Alps Wilderness (USFS), Siligo Peak (USGS), Caribou Lake (USGS).

SPECIAL CONSIDERATIONS: None.

PARKING AND FACILITIES: Bridge Camp Campground is located at the trailhead, which has horse facilities.

FINDING THE TRAILHEAD: From Weaverville, drive 12.9 miles north on Highway 3, then turn left (west) on County Road 112, a gravel road. Drive 4.1 miles to the end of the road.

From the trailhead, start out on the Stuart Fork Trail, which heads northwest up the canyon next to Stuart Fork Creek. Just above Oak Flat, the Bear Creek Trail comes up on the left, and the Stuart Fork Trail turns northward at a gradual bend in the main canyon. Just north of Cold Spring and the Deer Creek Trail junction, the canyon floor opens out into Morris Meadows, and the U-shaped, glacial character of the canyon becomes apparent. North of Morris Meadows, the canyon and trail begin to turn to the west, and the Caribou Scramble Trail forks right. The hike ends at the east end of Emerald Lake, a classic alpine lake set below craggy Sawtooth Ridge.

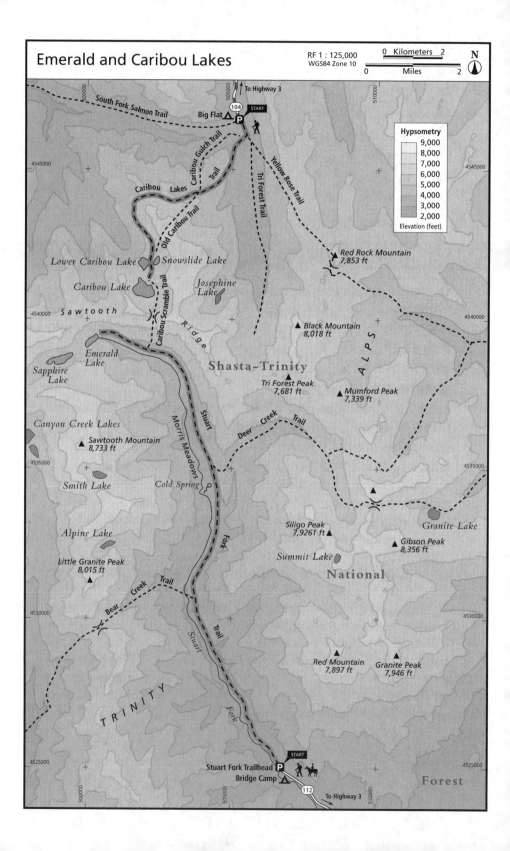

Emerald and Caribou Lakes

RF 1 : 125,000
WGS84 Zone 10

0   Kilometers   2

0   Miles   2

N

Hypsometry

9,000
8,000
7,000
6,000
5,000
4,000
3,000
2,000

Elevation (feet)

To Highway 3

South Fork Salmon Trail

Big Flat

104 START

Caribou Gulch Trail

Caribou   Lakes   Trail

Yellow Rose Trail

Tri Forest Trail

Old Caribou Trail

Lower Caribou Lake

Snowslide Lake

Red Rock Mountain
7,853 ft

Caribou Lake

Josephine
Lake

Caribou Scramble Trail

Sawtooth

Ridge

Black Mountain
8,018 ft

A L P S

Emerald
Lake

Shasta-Trinity

Sapphire
Lake

Tri Forest Peak
7,681 ft

Mumford Peak
7,339 ft

Canyon Creek Lakes

Morris Meadows

Stuart

Deer   Creek   Trail

Sawtooth Mountain
8,733 ft

Smith Lake

Cold Spring

Granite Lake

Alpine Lake

Siligo Peak
7,9261 ft

Gibson Peak
8,356 ft

Little Granite Peak
8,015 ft

Summit Lake

National

Bear   Creek   Trail

Fork

Trail

Red Mountain
7,897 ft

Granite Peak
7,946 ft

T R I N I T Y

Stuart

Fork

Trail

Stuart Fork Trailhead

Bridge Camp

START

112

To Highway 3

Forest

0.0 Stuart Fork Trailhead.

4.2 Bear Creek Trail on left; continue straight ahead on Stuart Fork Trail.

6.4 Cold Spring.

6.8 Deer Creek Trail on right; continue straight ahead on Stuart Fork Trail.

10.0 Caribou Scramble Trail on right; continue straight ahead on Stuart Fork Trail.

11.1 Emerald Lake.

Granite Lake

HIGHLIGHTS: A day or overnight hike to an easily accessible alpine lake.

TYPE OF TRIP: Out-and-back.

DISTANCE: 9.2 miles.

DIFFICULTY: Moderate.

PERMITTED USES: Hiking, horses.

MAPS: Trinity Alps Wilderness (USFS), Covington Mill (USGS).

SPECIAL CONSIDERATIONS: None.

PARKING AND FACILITIES: Dirt trailhead.

FINDING THE TRAILHEAD: From Trinity Center, drive 6.5 miles west on County Road 123, a gravel road, to the end of the road.

Start the hike on the Swift Creek Trail, which follows Swift Creek northwest up the deep, forested canyon. The first mile of the trail is in Preacher Meadow Research Natural Area. Research natural areas are established to protect unique areas for scientific study.

When Granite Creek comes in from the left, turn left on the Granite Lake Trail. This trail climbs gradually up the canyon to the southwest. Near the head of the canyon, the trail passes through Gibson Meadow before starting a steep ascent of the glacial headwall to Granite Lake. The lake is perched in a classic glacial cirque at the head of the canyon, below Gibson Peak.

KEY POINTS

0.0 Swift Creek Trailhead.

1.2 Turn left on Granite Lake Trail.

4.2 Gibson Meadow.

4.6 Granite Lake.

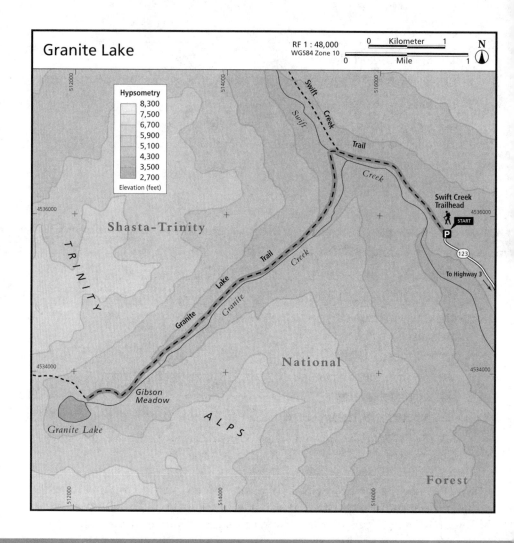

Granite Lake

RF 1 : 48,000
WGS84 Zone 10

0 _____ Kilometer _____ 1

0 _____ Mile _____ 1

N

Hypsometry
8,300
7,500
6,700
5,900
5,100
4,300
3,500
2,700
Elevation (feet)

Swift Creek

Swift

Creek Trail

Swift Creek
Trailhead

START

P

123

To Highway 3

Shasta-Trinity

TRINITY

Trail

Creek

Lake

Trail

Granite

Granite

Creek

National

Gibson
Meadow

ALPS

Granite Lake

Forest

Boulder Lake

HIGHLIGHTS: An easy day hike to a small alpine lake.

TYPE OF TRIP: Out-and-back.

DISTANCE: 3 miles.

DIFFICULTY: Easy.

PERMITTED USES: Hiking, horses.

MAPS: Trinity Alps Wilderness (USFS), Ycatapom Peak (USGS).

SPECIAL CONSIDERATIONS: None.

PARKING AND FACILITIES: Dirt trailhead parking.

Boulder Lake Trail, Trinity Alps.

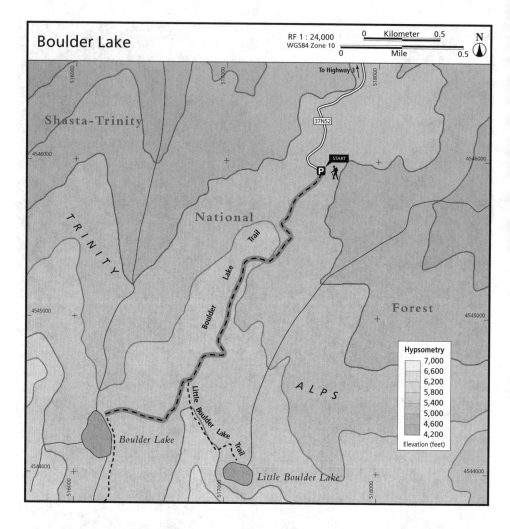

Boulder Lake

RF 1 : 24,000
WGS84 Zone 10

To Highway 3

37N52

START

P

Shasta-Trinity

National

Trail

TRINITY

Boulder

Lake

Forest

ALPS

Little Boulder Lake Trail

Boulder Lake

Little Boulder Lake

Hypsometry
7,000
6,600
6,200
5,800
5,400
5,000
4,600
4,200
Elevation (feet)

FINDING THE TRAILHEAD: From Trinity Center, drive 7.1 miles north on Highway 3, and then left (west) on Forest Road 37N52, a gravel road. Numerous logging roads branch off this road; stay on the main road 9.2 miles until its end.

The Boulder Lake Trail climbs very gradually southwest along the side of a ridge, passing through an old clear-cut before entering the wilderness area and old-growth forest. When the trail finally climbs onto the top of the ridge, the spur trail to Little Boulder Lake comes in from the left; stay right on Boulder Lake Trail. Turning westward, the trail descends slightly into the valley and reaches Boulder Lake, the goal for this hike.

KEY POINTS

0.0 Boulder Lake Trailhead.

0.9 Little Boulder Lake Trail; stay right on the Boulder Lake Trail.

1.5 Boulder Lake.

Caribou Lakes

See map on page 86.

HIGHLIGHTS: A long day or overnight hike to a group of scenic lakes set below rugged Sawtooth Ridge.

TYPE OF TRIP: Out-and-back.

DISTANCE: 14.6 miles.

DIFFICULTY: Difficult.

PERMITTED USES: Hiking, horses.

MAPS: Trinity Alps Wilderness (USFS), Caribou Lake (USGS).

SPECIAL CONSIDERATIONS: None.

PARKING AND FACILITIES: Mount Meadow Resort and Big Flat Campground are located near the trailhead.

FINDING THE TRAILHEAD: From Coffee Creek, drive 18.6 miles west and south on County Road 104 to the trailhead.

From Big Flat Trailhead, head south on the Caribou Lakes Trail. Almost immediately, you'll pass the Caribou Gulch and Tri Forest Trails; stay on the Caribou Lakes Trail, which ascends the west wall of the canyon in a series of switchbacks. More steady climbing leads to a long switchback. At the end of this switch, the trail crosses through a saddle, where the Caribou Gulch Trail comes in from the right and the Old Caribou Trail comes in from the left. Continue straight ahead on the Caribou Lakes Trail, which climbs gradually across the head of Big Conrad Gulch. A few more switchbacks lead to a saddle near Browns Meadow. Here the trail turns south along west-facing slopes and climbs gradually to meet the south end of the Old Caribou Trail. Stay right on the Caribou Lakes Trail, which now descends a few hundred feet to Snowshoe Lake, which the trail passes on its west side. A final short climb leads to Caribou Lake, set in a spectacular cirque below Sawtooth Ridge.

0.0   Big Flat Trailhead.

0.1   Caribou Gulch Trail on right; continue straight ahead (south) on Caribou Lakes Trail.

0.2   Tri Forest Trail goes left; stay right on Caribou Lakes Trail.

2.8   Caribou Gulch Trail on right and Old Caribou Trail on left; continue straight on Caribou Lakes Trail.

6.5   Old Caribou Trail on left; continue straight on Caribou Lakes Trail.

7.3   Caribou Lakes.

Stoddard Lake

HIGHLIGHTS: A moderate day hike to a pair of lakes in a scenic alpine setting.

TYPE OF TRIP: Out-and-back.

DISTANCE: 6.2 miles.

DIFFICULTY: Moderate.

PERMITTED USES: Hiking, horses.

MAPS: Trinity Alps Wilderness (USFS), Tangle Blue Lake (USGS), Billys Peak (USGS).

SPECIAL CONSIDERATIONS: None.

PARKING AND FACILITIES: Dirt trailhead.

FINDING THE TRAILHEAD: From the town of Coffee Creek, drive 2.4 miles north on Highway 3, and turn left (west) on County Road 135, the Eagle Creek Loop, which is a gravel road. Drive 1.2 miles, then turn left (west) on Forest Road 38N22. Drive 5.2 miles to the trailhead.

The Stoddard Lake Trail starts out by climbing west up a forested ridge, but it soon leaves the ridge to climb gradually across the slopes to the north. After passing through an unnamed saddle, the Stoddard Lake Trail descends into a broad basin containing Stoddard Meadow and the junction with the East Fork Coffee Creek Trail. Turn left to stay on the Stoddard Lake Trail, which now heads south and climbs up a gentle slope to reach the north shore of Stoddard Lake, the goal for the hike. A smaller lake, McDonald Lake, is just above Stoddard Lake to the south.

Stoddard and Big Bear Lakes

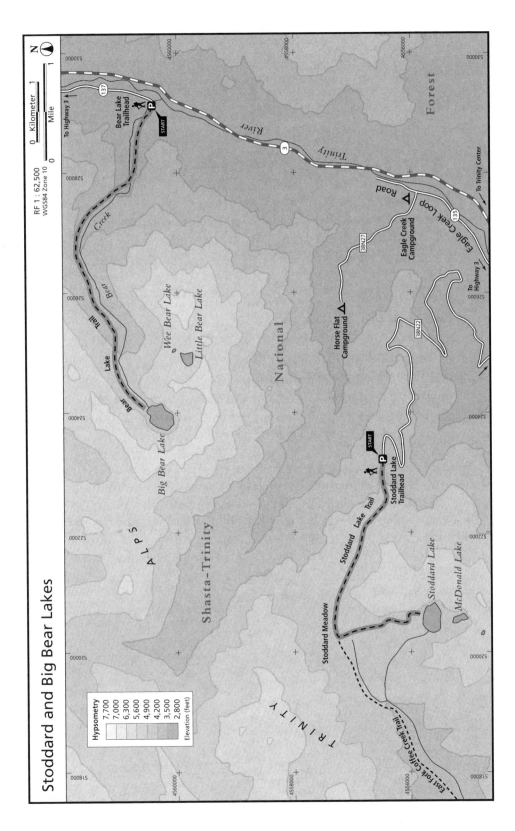

See map on page 93.

KEY POINTS

0.0   Stoddard Lake Trailhead.
1.6   Saddle.
2.1   East Fork Coffee Creek Trail; turn left to stay on Stoddard Lake Trail.
3.1   Stoddard Lake.

Big Bear Lake

See map on page 93.

HIGHLIGHTS: A day hike to an alpine lake, from a trailhead easily accessible from Highway 3.

TYPE OF TRIP: Out-and-back.

DISTANCE: 7.6 miles.

DIFFICULTY: Moderate.

PERMITTED USES: Hiking, horses.

MAPS: Trinity Alps Wilderness (USFS), Tangle Blue Lake (USGS).

SPECIAL CONSIDERATIONS: None.

PARKING AND FACILITIES: Dirt trailhead.

FINDING THE TRAILHEAD: From the town of Coffee Creek, drive 10.2 miles north on Highway 3, then turn left on County Road 137, a gravel road. Drive north 0.8 mile to the trailhead.

From the trailhead next to the Trinity River, the Bear Lake Trail heads west up Bear Creek, climbing steadily. The gradient is moderate but unrelenting as the trail generally follows the creek, all the way to Big Bear Lake. Your reward for this long climb is a view of Big Bear Lake in its glacial cirque surrounded by cliffs and a craggy skyline.

KEY POINTS

0.0   Bear Lake Trailhead.
3.8   Big Bear Lake.

Shasta Lake Unit: Whiskeytown–Shasta– Trinity National Recreation Area

he Shasta Lake Unit encompasses Shasta Lake, the largest reservoir in the national recreation area. Formed by Shasta Dam, at 602 feet tall and 3,460 feet long, the second-largest concrete dam in the country, Shasta Lake covers 30,000 acres and is 517 feet deep when full and more than 30 miles long. Shasta Dam was built between 1938 and 1945, and the resulting reservoir is the largest in California. Shasta Lake provides water and power to the Central Valley via the Central Valley Project. Since water releases are tied to the needs of the downstream users, Shasta Lake is subject to heavy drawdown, especially in late summer. This fact, coupled with the sheer size of the lake, makes it the domain of houseboaters, powerboaters, and water-skiers. On the other hand, there are plenty of quiet coves far from the developed areas of the lake that are pleasant destinations for paddlers and anglers.

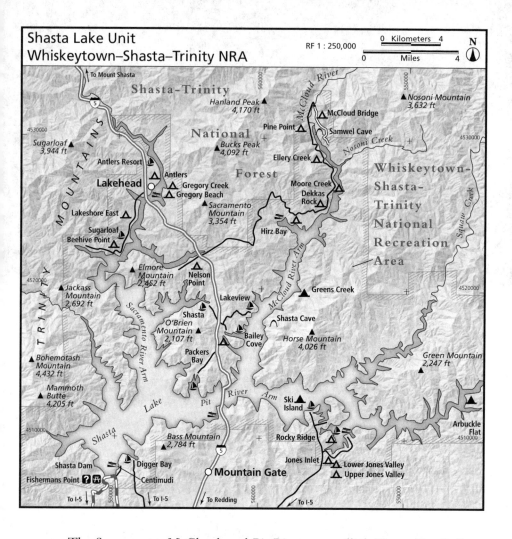

Shasta Lake Unit
Whiskeytown–Shasta–Trinity NRA

RF 1 : 250,000

0 Kilometers 4

0 Miles 4

N

To Mount Shasta

Shasta-Trinity

Hanland Peak ▲
4,170 ft

Nosoni Mountain ▲
3,632 ft

McCloud River

McCloud Bridge ▲

Pine Point △

Samwel Cave ▲

National

Bucks Peak
4,092 ft

Nosoni Creek

Whiskeytown–
Shasta–
Trinity
National
Recreation
Area

Sugarloaf ▲
3,944 ft

Antlers Resort ⚓

Ellery Creek △

Forest

Moore Creek △

Squaw Creek

Lakehead ○

Antlers △

Gregory Creek △

Gregory Beach △

Dekkas
Rock △

Lakeshore East △

Sacramento
Mountain ▲
3,354 ft

Hirz Bay

Sugarloaf
Beehive Point △

Jackass
Mountain ▲
2,692 ft

Elmore
Mountain ▲
2,452 ft

Nelson △
Point

Lakeview

McCloud River Arm

Greens Creek ▲

Green Mountain ▲
2,247 ft

Shasta
O'Brien
Mountain ▲
2,107 ft

Shasta Cave △

Sacramento River Arm

Bailey
Cove

Horse Mountain ▲
4,026 ft

Bohemotash
Mountain ▲
4,432 ft

Packers
Bay

Mammoth
Butte ▲
4,205 ft

Lake

Shasta

Pit

River

Arm

Ski ▲
Island

Arbuckle
Flat

Bass Mountain ▲
2,784 ft

Rocky Ridge △

Jones Inlet

Lower Jones Valley △

Upper Jones Valley △

Shasta Dam

Digger Bay

Mountain Gate ○

Fishermans Point

Centimudi

To I-5

To I-5

To Redding

To I-5

The Sacramento, McCloud, and Pit Rivers, as well as Squaw Creek, flow
into the lake, creating four major arms, each with its own character. There are
five major developed areas on the lake, each featuring boat ramps, marinas,
campgrounds, and private resorts.

The Sacramento River Arm is the major arm of the lake. There are two
main developed areas: Lakehead, at the north end of the Sacramento River
Arm, is easily accessible from Interstate 5. Shasta Dam is reached from I–5
north of Redding via Highway 151 and Digger Bay Boulevard. Under the
waters of the lake lies the Oregon Trail, a major emigrant trail used from 1834,
when it was first used by Michael La Framboise, a Hudson Bay Company trapper, until the construction of the Central Pacific Railroad in 1872. Trappers,
then gold rush prospectors, and still later, emigrants, used the Oregon Trail to

travel between San Francisco and Oregon's Willamette Valley. An old mining town, Kennett, now lies under 400 feet of water just upstream of Shasta Dam. Kennett was founded during the gold rush and boomed in the early part of the twentieth century. When copper prices fell after World War I, Kennett fell on hard times.

At Shasta Dam, at the south end of the Sacramento River Arm, the Bureau of Land Management operates the Shasta Dam Visitor Center. North of the dam lies the broadest and most open portion of Shasta Lake, set off by towering volcanoes, Mount Shasta and Lassen Peak. Shasta Dam Vista offers a panoramic view of the lake, the dam, and the mountains. A picnic area and public boat ramp are nearby, as well as Digger Bay Marina. Shasta Marina is located just off I–5 at the head of O'Brien Creek Inlet, which enters the Sacramento River Arm on the east side about midway up the length of the arm. At the north end of the Sacramento River Arm, the Lakehead area is the most developed and busiest area on Shasta Lake. I–5 bisects the Lakehead area and offers easy access. There are U.S. Forest Service and private campgrounds, public boat ramps, marinas, and many private cottages, lodges, and resorts.

Named for Alexander McCloud, a Scottish trapper who overwintered along the river in 1829, the McCloud River drains into what is now the McCloud River Arm of Shasta Lake. There are two main developed areas along this arm: the Lower McCloud area, which is reached via the O'Brien Exit from I–5, and the Upper McCloud area at the north end of the arm. This more remote area is reached via Gilman Road from I–5. Both areas along the McCloud Arm have hiking and mountain-biking trails, U.S. Forest Service and private campgrounds, as well as public boat ramps, marinas, and private resorts.

An added attraction of the Lower McCloud area is Shasta Caverns, a natural limestone cave with extensive decorations. Commercially operated, Shasta Caverns offers tours hourly during the summer. Contact Lake Shasta Caverns at (916) 238–2341 or www.lakeshastacaverns.com.

Samwel Cave is located near the head of the McCloud River Arm on its east side. Because of vandalism, the public may only enter the entrance room of the cave. Qualified cavers may obtain a permit from the U.S. Forest Service to explore the rest of the cave. A nature trail leads to the entrance.

Pit River Arm is the longest arm of Lake Shasta and is crossed by I–5 via the highest double–decker bridge in the country. Two large marinas, Packers Bay and Bridge Bay Resort, service the lower Pit River Arm. Midway up the Pit River Arm on the south side, the Jones Valley area offers two marinas, public boat ramps, and several U.S. Forest Service campgrounds. The Jones Valley areas is accessed via I–5 and the Oasis Road Exit to Bear Mountain Road. The long and narrow Upper Pit River Arm is undeveloped and is accessible only by boat or rough, unmaintained dirt roads.

The Squaw Creek Arm branches off the Pit River Arm on its north side. Like the Upper Pit River Arm, the Squaw Creek Arm is accessible only by boat or unmaintained dirt roads. Both of these quiet arms are popular with houseboaters, anglers, and others looking for a more quiet section of Shasta Lake.

Visitor Centers and Amenities

The Shasta Lake Unit is administered by the U.S. Forest Service, which operates the Shasta Visitor Center in Redding. At the visitor center, maps, books, and up-to-date information can be obtained.

Campgrounds

As the most developed of the four lakes in the national recreation area, Shasta Lake has plenty of public campgrounds, all operated by the U.S. Forest Service.

The following auto-accessible campgrounds are located on the Sacramento River Arm of Shasta Lake.

Nelson Point Campground is located on the Salt Creek Road west of I–5, on Salt Creek Inlet. It has eight units and no water.

Lakeshore East Campground is located on the west side of the Sacramento River Arm south of Lakeshore Resort. It is reached from I–5 via Lakeshore Drive. It has twenty-six units.

Beehive Point Campground is at the south end of Lakeshore Drive, off I–5, on the west shore of the Sacramento River Arm. It has shoreline camping instead of designated sites and no water.

Gregory Beach Campground on the east side of the Sacramento River Arm is reached via Gregory Creek Road off I–5. It has shoreline camping without formal designated units and no water.

Gregory Creek Campground is also on the east side of the Sacramento River Arm at the end of Gregory Creek Road, off I–5. It has eighteen units.

Antlers Campground is on the west side of the Sacramento River Arm, off I–5 at the end of Antlers Road. It is wheelchair-accessible and has fifty-nine units.

Bailey Cove Campground is just off I–5 on the lower McCloud River Arm and is reached via Shasta Caverns Road and Bailey Cove Road. It has seven units, a picnic area, and features the Bailey Cove Trail.

The following campgrounds are located on the upper McCloud River Arm of Shasta Lake. To reach this area, exit I–5 onto Gilman Road.

Hirz Bay Campground is south of Gilman Road on Hirz Bay, on the west side of the upper McCloud River Arm. It has forty-eight units, a boat ramp, and features the east end of the Hirz Bay Trail. There is also a group campground.

Bailey Cove Trail, Shasta Lake.

Dekkas Rock Group Campground is a group of campgrounds on the west side of the upper McCloud River Arm, off Gilman Road.

Moore Creek Campground is on the west shore of the upper McCloud River Arm, on Gilman Road. It has twelve units.

Ellery Creek Campground is also on the west shore of the upper McCloud River Arm, on Gilman Road. It has nineteen units.

Pine Point Campground is on the west shore of the McCloud River Arm near its head, on Gilman Road. It has fourteen units and is wheelchair-accessible.

McCloud Bridge Campground is on the east shore of the McCloud River Arm near its head. From the north end of Gilman Road, cross the McCloud River Bridge onto Fenders Ferry Road, and take an immediate right into the campground. The campground has fourteen units and is wheelchair-accessible.

The final group of auto-accessible campgrounds on Shasta Lake are located in the Jones Valley area on the middle Pit River Arm, which is reached via Bear Mountain Road from I–5.

Jones Inlet Campground is located on the south side of Jones Valley Bay off Jones Valley Road. It has shoreline camping, drinking water, and no designated units.

Lower Jones Valley Campground is on the south side of Jones Valley Bay off Jones Valley Road. It has thirteen units.

Upper Jones Valley Campground is next to Lower Jones Valley Campground. It has eight units.

Finally, there are several boat-in campgrounds on Shasta Lake, accessible only from the water. These include **Gooseneck Cove, Greens Creek, Ski Island,** and **Arbuckle Flat**. None of these campgrounds have piped water. In addition, boaters are free to camp elsewhere along the lakeshore, except in areas closed to camping. A California campfire permit is required for both campfires and camp stoves outside designated campgrounds, and can be obtained free from any U.S. Forest Service ranger station.

Fishing

Fishing from both lakeshore and boat is popular on Shasta Lake. Species include silver salmon; brown and rainbow trout; sturgeon; brown, white, channel, and bullhead catfish; bluegill; green sunfish; and spotted, smallmouth, and largemouth bass.

The California Department of Fish and Game regulates fishing, and a valid fishing license is required. Check with the department for current fishing regulations.

Water Sports

Boat rentals, including houseboats, various types of powerboats, rowboats, canoes, and kayaks, are available from several of the marinas on Shasta Lake. Check with marinas ahead of time and make reservations, especially during holiday periods. The U.S. Forest Service can supply a list of the current commercial operators on the lake.

Waterskiing is very popular on Shasta Lake, especially in the Jones Valley Area on the Pit River Arm and along the Sacramento River Arm. Waterskiing is not recommended on the upper Pit River Arm because snags and debris are present. In addition, waterskiing is not allowed on the Pit River Arm above Browns Canyon, on the Sacramento River Arm above Middle Salt Creek Inlet, and in several smaller inlets and coves as marked by buoys.

Although there are no designated swim areas or beaches on Shasta Lake, swimming from boats or the shore is popular during the summer months. Swimming is prohibited at boat ramps and in the main channels. Never swim alone or in areas with boat traffic, and always check for underwater obstacles before diving.

Several public boat ramps provide access to Shasta Lake. Some ramps become unusable at lower lake levels or when blocked by debris. There is a fee for the use of most boat ramps.

Centimudi Boat Ramp is near Shasta Dam at the end of Kennett Road. It is usable to 210 feet below maximum pool.

Sugarloaf Boat Ramp is on the west side of the upper Sacramento River Arm along Lakeshore Drive west of I–5. It is usable to 160 feet below maximum pool.

Packers Bay Boat Ramp is located at Packers Bay Marina west of I–5, at the end of Packers Bay Road. It is usable to 115 feet below maximum pool.

Bailey Cove Boat Ramp is located near Bailey Cove Campground on the lower McCloud River Arm off I–5 on Shasta Caverns and Bailey Cove Roads. It is usable to 50 feet below maximum pool.

Hirz Bay Boat Ramp is on Gilman Road on the west side of the upper McCloud River Arm, at Hirz Bay Group Campground. It is usable to 115 feet below maximum pool.

Jones Valley Boat Ramp is at the end of Jones Valley Road in the Jones Valley Area, on the south side of the Pit River Arm. It is usable to 210 feet below maximum pool.

Trails

Hiking trails are limited in the Shasta Lake area. A much more extensive network of trails for the day hiker, as well as the equestrian and backpacker, is found just north of Shasta Lake at Castle Crags State Park and Castle Crags Wilderness Area.

Bailey Cove Trail

HIGHLIGHTS: An easy loop around a large peninsula, featuring views of the Bailey Cove area as well as the lower McCloud River Arm of Shasta Lake.

TYPE OF TRIP: Loop.

DISTANCE: 2.4 miles.

DIFFICULTY: Easy.

PERMITTED USES: Hiking, mountain biking.

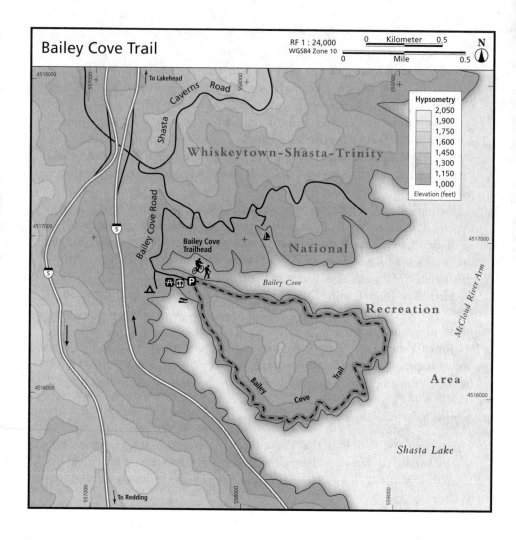

MAPS: Whiskeytown–Shasta–Trinity National Recreation Area (Earthwalk Press), O'Brien (USGS).

SPECIAL CONSIDERATIONS: Since lake levels vary considerably, the actual lakeshore may be well below the trail.

PARKING AND FACILITIES: Bailey Cove Day Use Area and Picnic Area.

FINDING THE TRAILHEAD: From Interstate 5, exit at Shasta Caverns Road, drive 0.3 mile east on Shasta Caverns, then turn right on Bailey Cove Road. Drive to the end of the road and park in the Bailey Cove Day Use Area.

The Bailey Cove Trail can be ridden or hiked in either direction, since it is nearly level. This description follows the trail clockwise, starting on the north side. Here the trail runs through dense forest, which favors the cool, shady north-facing slopes. After passing the marina in Bailey Cove, the trail reaches a viewpoint at the easternmost point of the peninsula, which offers a great view up and down the lower McCloud River Arm of Shasta Lake. As the trail reaches the south-facing slopes and turns west, note how oak and manzanita dominate this much drier slope. Wild grape and poison oak are common along the trail.

KEY POINTS

0.0 Bailey Cove Trailhead.

0.9 Viewpoint overlooking McCloud River Arm.

2.4 Bailey Cove Trailhead.

Hirz Bay Trail

HIGHLIGHTS: This trail follows the shoreline in the upper McCloud River Arm of Shasta Lake.

TYPE OF TRIP: Out-and-back.

DISTANCE: 2.6 miles.

DIFFICULTY: Easy.

PERMITTED USES: Hiking, mountain biking.

MAPS: Whiskeytown–Shasta–Trinity National Recreation Area (Earthwalk Press), Bollibokka Mountain (USGS), Minnesota Mountain (USGS).

SPECIAL CONSIDERATIONS: There is no trailhead parking at Hirz Bay Group Campground, so it is best to park at Dekkas Rock Group Campground.

PARKING AND FACILITIES: Dekkas Rock Day Use Area.

FINDING THE TRAILHEAD: Exit Interstate 5 at Gilman Road, then drive 8.6 miles east on Gilman Road to Dekkas Rock Group Campground. Park in the day-use area on the right, before entering the campground.

This easy and scenic trail follows the shoreline of the McCloud River Arm from Dekkas Rock Group Campground to Hirz Bay Group Campground, generally staying just above the high water line of Shasta Lake. When the lake is drawn

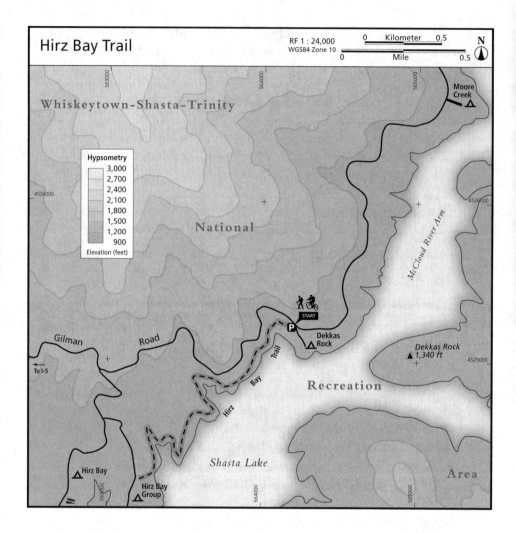

down, the actual lakeshore may be well below the trail, but several informal side trails lead down to the shoreline.

KEY POINTS

0.0 Dekkas Rock Trailhead.

1.3 Hirz Bay Group Campground.

Hirz Bay Trail, Shasta Lake.

Castle Crags

Castle Crags is a prominent area of sharp, jagged peaks rising east of the Sacramento River Valley. This small but rugged area contains numerous 6,000-foot, glacier-carved peaks, steep canyons, and a few alpine lakes. Much of the Castle Crags area is covered by rocky outcrops and brushfields. North- and east-facing slopes are covered with a mixed conifer forest. Some of the creek headwaters have wet, alpine meadows. Several trails traverse the 10,500-acre Castle Crags Wilderness Area, including a portion of the Pacific Crest National Scenic Trail. A more extensive trail network is found in the adjoining Castle Crags State Park.

A part of the Klamath Mountains, Castle Crags is formed from a granite pluton that intruded into the region's more common volcanic and sedimentary rocks. Although no icefields or glaciers are found in the Castle Crags at present, extensive glacial features prove that ice was a major factor in carving the present landscape.

Native Americans occupied the river valley below Castle Crags for thousands of years. As elsewhere in California, the coming of the gold rush resulted in rapid changes in the area, as hordes of miners arrived. Conflicts between miners and natives resulted in the Battle of Castle Crags, fought near Battle Rock and Castle Lake in 1855. This battle marked the beginning of the long Modoc War. In 1866 the railroad was finished along the Sacramento River, which opened up the area to heavy mining and logging operations. Numerous

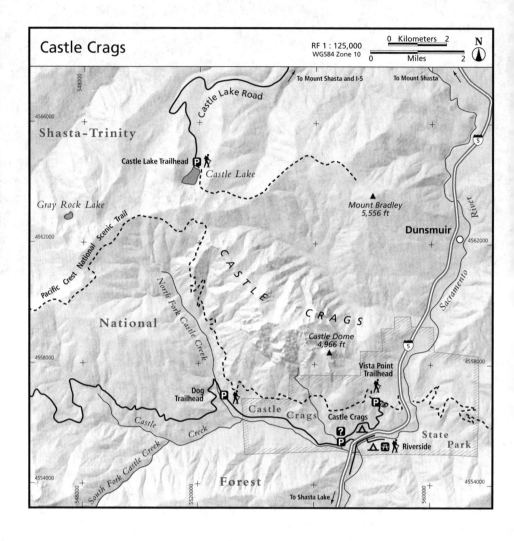

Castle Crags

RF 1 : 125,000
WGS84 Zone 10

resorts sprang up in the early twentieth century, many located at mineral springs. Concerned that this dramatic landscape would soon be irreparably scarred, in 1933 concerned citizens succeeded in acquiring the land that would eventually become the state park. Castle Crags Wilderness, created by Congress in 1984, added further protection to the area.

Visitor Centers and Amenities

The Castle Crags State Park entrance station has a small visitor center, which is reached by taking the Castella Exit and Castle Creek Road from Interstate 5.

Castle Crags.

Campgrounds

Castle Crags Campground is located west of I–5 in the state park, beyond the entrance station. It has 64 units.

Riverside Campground is located east of I–5, along the Sacramento River in the state park, and can be reached by taking the Frontage Road north to the campground turnoff. It has twelve units.

Sims Flat Campground is south of Castle Crags State Park on the east side of I–5 at the Sims Exit. It has twenty sites and is wheelchair-accessible.

Scenic Drives

Within the state park, a short but very narrow and winding road leads through the main campground and up to a vista point. A short walk leads to the viewpoint itself, which has views of both Castle Crags and Mount Shasta.

Finding the Trailheads

The Entrance Station Trailhead has a large parking lot and restrooms located just south of the state park entrance station and visitor center. It provides access to the Indian Creek Nature Trail, the Campground Trail, and the Flume Trail.

Riverside Trailhead is located in the Riverside Day Use Area, which is reached by taking Frontage and Riverside Roads from the Castella Exit on I–5. It provides day-use access to the River Trail, which can also be accessed from the lower loop of Castle Crags Campground.

Vista Point Trailhead is located at the end of the Vista Point Road, beyond Castle Crags Campground, and provides access to the Root Creek and Castle Dome Trails, as well as the Pacific Crest National Scenic Trail.

Dog Trailhead is reached from the Castella Exit on I–5 by driving 7 miles west on Castle Creek Road. It provides access to the Dog Trail and the Pacific Crest National Scenic Trail.

Castle Lake Trailhead is on the north side of the Castle Crags Wilderness and is reached from the town of Mount Shasta. From downtown Mount Shasta, drive 0.6 mile south on South Mount Shasta Boulevard, where Mount Shasta Boulevard turns left. Continue straight ahead (south) onto Ream Avenue. After crossing under I–5, turn left on WA Barr Road. Drive 2.2 miles, then turn left on Castle Lake Road. Continue 7.2 miles to the end of the road. From this trailhead, you can access the Castle Shore and Castle Lake Trails.

Trails

Indian Creek Nature Trail

HIGHLIGHTS: An interpretive trail that crosses Indian Creek twice.

TYPE OF TRIP: Loop.

DISTANCE: 1 mile.

DIFFICULTY: Easy.

PERMITTED USES: Hiking.

MAPS: Castle Crags Wilderness (USFS), Dunsmuir (USGS).

SPECIAL CONSIDERATIONS: Dogs are not allowed.

PARKING AND FACILITIES: Gravel parking lot with restrooms.

FINDING THE TRAILHEAD: From Interstate 5, take the Castella Exit and go west on Castle Creek Road to Castle Crags State Park. The trailhead is the large gravel parking lot south of the entrance station and visitor center.

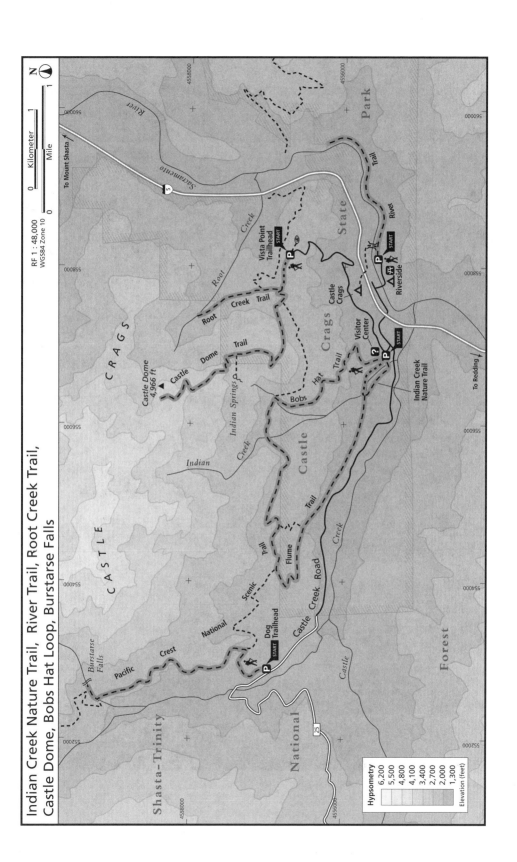

Indian Creek Nature Trail, River Trail, Root Creek Trail, Castle Dome, Bobs Hat Loop, Burstarse Falls

RF 1 : 48,000
WGS84 Zone 10

Water ditch, Indian Creek Nature Trail.

The trail starts near the entrance to the parking lot, and a trail guide brochure is available from a box. Meandering through cool and shady forest, the trail crosses Indian Creek twice on footbridges. Several points offer distant views of Castle Crags. This is a good trail for spring wildflower viewing.

River Trail

See map on page 111.

HIGHLIGHTS: A delightful walk along a quiet section of the Sacramento River.

TYPE OF TRIP: Out-and-back.

DISTANCE: 2.8 miles.

DIFFICULTY: Easy.

PERMITTED USES: Hiking.

MAPS: Castle Crags Wilderness (USFS), Dunsmuir (USGS).

SPECIAL CONSIDERATIONS: Dogs are not allowed.

PARKING AND FACILITIES: Riverside Campground and Picnic Area, restrooms.

FINDING THE TRAILHEAD: From Interstate 5, take the Castella Exit, then turn north on Frontage Road to Riverside Road. If you are staying in Castle Crags Campground, you can access the River Trail from the lower loop. This 0.4-mile spur trail crosses a footbridge over the Sacramento River to join the River Trail 0.1 mile from Riverside Trailhead.

The River Trail follows the east bank of the Sacramento River past the spur trail to Castle Crags Campground. The suspension bridge is a great place to enjoy views of the river. The trail crosses two permanent creeks and offers great spring wildflowers and fall colors.

KEY POINTS

0.0 Riverside Trailhead.

0.1 Bridge and trail to Castle Crags Campground.

1.4 End of trail.

Root Creek Trail

See map on page 111.

HIGHLIGHTS: A gentle, easy hike to Root Creek .

TYPE OF TRIP: Out-and-back.

DISTANCE: 2 miles.

DIFFICULTY: Easy.

PERMITTED USES: Hiking.

MAPS: Castle Crags Wilderness (USFS), Dunsmuir (USGS).

SPECIAL CONSIDERATIONS: Dogs are not allowed.

PARKING AND FACILITIES: Paved Vista Point parking lot, restrooms.

FINDING THE TRAILHEAD: From the Castle Crags State Park entrance station, continue on the main park road, through the campground, to the end of the road.

Start on the Castle Dome Trail, then turn right onto the Root Creek Trail. Walking is easy, and the entire trail is shaded by deep, mixed conifer forest. During the spring and early summer, a bonus is the many varieties of orchids blooming along the trail. The trail ends at beautiful Root Creek.

KEY POINTS

0.0   Vista Point Trailhead.

0.3   Turn right on Root Creek Trail.

1.0   Root Creek.

Castle Dome

See map on page 111.

HIGHLIGHTS: The end of this rugged trail offers great views, and a spur trail leads to delightful Indian Springs.

TYPE OF TRIP: Out-and-back.

DISTANCE: 5.2 miles.

DIFFICULTY: Difficult.

PERMITTED USES: Hiking.

MAPS: Castle Crags Wilderness (USFS), Dunsmuir (USGS).

SPECIAL CONSIDERATIONS: Dogs are not allowed.

PARKING AND FACILITIES: Paved Vista Point parking lot, restrooms.

FINDING THE TRAILHEAD: From the Castle Crags State Park entrance station, continue on the main park road, through the campground, to the end of the road.

Start on the Castle Dome Trail, which climbs gradually west along a heavily forested ridge to meet the Root Creek Trail. Continue on the Castle Dome Trail, which now begins to climb steeply. At a saddle, a spur trail goes left 0.2 mile to Indian Spring, a worthwhile side trip that adds 0.4 mile to the total hike distance. Resuming the steep ascent, the Castle Dome Trail soon emerges from the forest onto open, brushy slopes and climbs steeply to end on the rocky ridge west of Castle Dome and the end of the hike. The ascent of Castle Dome itself requires technical rock-climbing skills and equipment.

KEY POINTS

0.0 Vista Point Trailhead.

0.3 Root Creek Trail forks right; continue straight ahead on Castle Dome Trail.

1.5 Side trail to Indian Spring on left.

2.6 End of trail on ridge west of Castle Dome.

Bobs Hat Loop

See map on page 111.

HIGHLIGHTS: A good hike in spring, when the wildflowers are out and the seasonal creeks are running, and also in winter, when higher trails are snow-covered.

TYPE OF TRIP: Loop.

DISTANCE: 5.5 miles.

DIFFICULTY: Moderate.

PERMITTED USES: Hiking.

MAPS: Castle Crags Wilderness (USFS), Dunsmuir (USGS).

SPECIAL CONSIDERATIONS: Dogs are not allowed.

PARKING AND FACILITIES: Gravel parking lot with restrooms.

FINDING THE TRAILHEAD: From Interstate 5, take the Castella Exit and go west on Castle Creek Road to Castle Crags State Park. The trailhead is the large gravel parking lot south of the entrance station and visitor center.

Start the hike on the Indian Creek Nature Trail, which is a loop. Stay right when the loop begins. At the west end of the loop, turn right on the Flume Trail. This trail follows a water flume and ditch system that used to bring water to the town of Castella. A spur trail goes right and climbs to the Pacific Crest National Scenic Trail; stay left here and continue on the Flume Trail for a gentler ascent to the Pacific Crest Trail farther west. When the main Flume Trail ends at the Pacific Crest Trail, turn right and follow the Pacific Crest Trail east across the slope. You'll pass the spur trail to the Flume Trail on the right; stay on the Pacific Crest Trail and continue east to the Bobs Hat Trail. Turn right onto the Bobs Hat Trail and descend to the Entrance Station Trailhead.

KEY POINTS

0.0 Entrance Station Trailhead.

0.4 Turn right on Flume Trail.

1.6 Spur trail on right to Pacific Crest Trail; continue on Flume Trail.

2.4 Pacific Crest National Scenic Trail; turn right (east).

2.9 Spur trail on right to Flume Trail; continue on Pacific Crest Trail.

4.2 Turn right (south) on Bobs Hat Trail.

5.5 Entrance Station Trailhead.

Burstarse Falls

See map on page 111.

HIGHLIGHTS: This hike uses the Dog and Pacific Crest Trails to reach Burstarse Falls, which is best in spring and early summer.

TYPE OF TRIP: Out-and-back.

DISTANCE: 4.4 miles.

DIFFICULTY: Moderate.

PERMITTED USES: Hiking.

MAPS: Castle Crags Wilderness (USFS), Dunsmuir (USGS).

SPECIAL CONSIDERATIONS: The trail is in the Shasta–Trinity National Forest, and dogs are allowed.

PARKING AND FACILITIES: Dirt parking area.

FINDING THE TRAILHEAD: From the Castella Exit on Interstate 5, drive 7 miles west on Castle Creek Road to the Dog Trailhead.

From the trailhead, follow the Dog Trail up a steep, south-facing slope to meet the Pacific Crest National Scenic Trail. Turn left and follow the Pacific Crest Trail to the crossing of Burstarse Creek. Leave the trail and walk up the creek past a small falls and a cascade to the 40-foot main fall.

KEY POINTS

0.0 Dog Trailhead.

0.5 Pacific Crest National Scenic Trail; turn left.

2.1 Burstarse Creek; turn right and walk up the creek.

2.2 Burstarse Falls.

Little Castle Lake

HIGHLIGHTS: A hike past the largest lake in the Castle Crags to a small lake with a great view of Mount Shasta.

TYPE OF TRIP: Out-and-back.

DISTANCE: 1.8 miles.

DIFFICULTY: Easy.

PERMITTED USES: Hiking, horses.

MAPS: Castle Crags Wilderness (USFS), Seven Lakes Basin (USGS), Dunsmuir (USGS).

SPECIAL CONSIDERATIONS: The trail is in the Shasta–Trinity National Forest, and dogs are allowed.

PARKING AND FACILITIES: Paved parking lot and day-use area with restrooms.

FINDING THE TRAILHEAD: From downtown Mount Shasta, drive 0.6 mile south on South Mount Shasta Boulevard, where Mount Shasta Boulevard turns left. Continue straight ahead (south) onto Ream Avenue. After crossing under Interstate 5, turn left on WA Barr Road. Drive 2.2 miles, then turn left on Castle Lake Road. Continue 7.2 miles to the end of the road.

From the trailhead, start out on the Castle Lake Trail, which climbs south up the slopes on the east side of Castle Lake. The trail soon crosses an unnamed pass and descends to tiny Little Castle Lake.

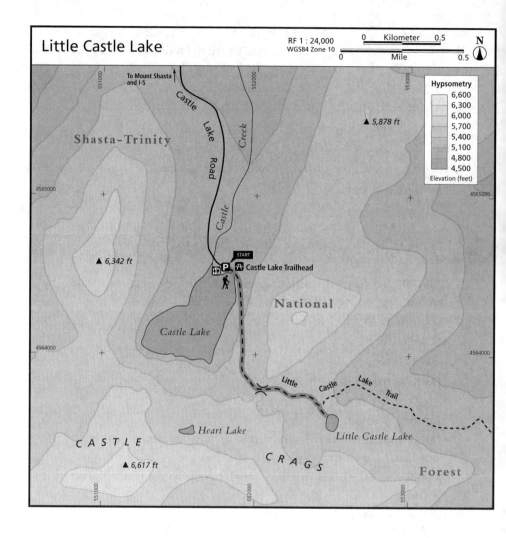

Little Castle Lake

RF 1 : 24,000
WGS84 Zone 10

Hypsometry

	Elevation (feet)
	6,600
	6,300
	6,000
	5,700
	5,400
	5,100
	4,800
	4,500

KEY POINTS

0.0 Castle Lake Trailhead.

0.6 Pass.

0.9 Little Castle Lake.

Mount Shasta and the Medicine Lake Highlands

ount Shasta is the crowning glory of the Shasta region and the area's most prominent landmark. At 14,162 feet, it is the second highest of the volcanoes in the Cascade Range and is visible for hundreds of miles. Although not the highest, it is the largest in volume of the Cascade volcanoes. The mountain rises more than 10,000 feet above its base and creates its own weather. In fact, Mount Shasta is famous for its dramatic lenticular clouds that often form when high winds blow over the summit. Pacific storms drop large amounts of snow on the mountain throughout the winter season, and there are seven named glaciers—Whitney, Konwakiton, Wintun, Hotlum, Bolam, Watkins, and Mud Creek—draping the slopes below the summit. Mount Shasta is a stratovolcano, formed by successive flows of lava, pyroclastic materials, and debris flows. The present mountain was formed by four distinct periods of volcanic activity, from four different main vents, starting about 200,000 to 300,000 years ago. The fourth eruptive period started about 9,700 years ago and is probably still active, since the last eruption was in 1786. Although modified by erosion, Shasta still has the classic stratovolcano shape, especially when seen from a distance.

In 1984 Congress added Mount Shasta to the National Wilderness Preservation System. Mount Shasta Wilderness Area covers 38,200 acres and has

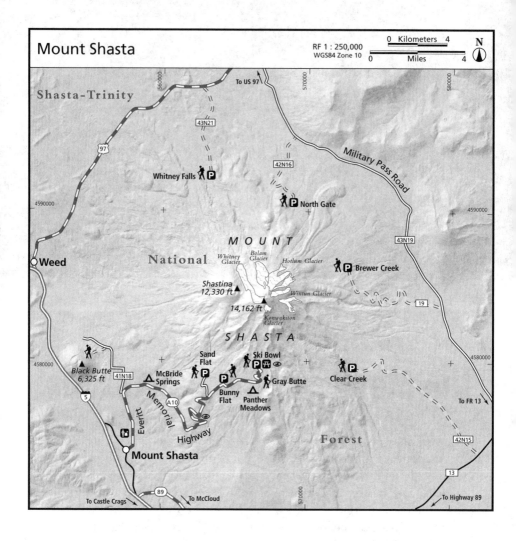

Mount Shasta

RF 1 : 250,000
WGS84 Zone 10

0 Kilometers 4
0 Miles 4

N

Shasta-Trinity

To US 97

43N21

42N16

Military Pass Road

97

Whitney Falls P

North Gate P

43N19

Weed

National

M O U N T

Whitney Glacier
Bolam Glacier
Hotlum Glacier

Brewer Creek P

Shastina 12,330 ft ▲

Wintun Glacier

14,162 ft ▲

19

Konwakiton Glacier

S H A S T A

Sand Flat

Ski Bowl

Black Butte 6,325 ft ▲

41N18

McBride Springs

P

P

Gray Butte

Clear Creek P

4580000

5

Everitt

Memorial

A10

Bunny Flat

Panther Meadows

To FR 13

Highway

Forest

42N15

Mount Shasta

13

89

To Castle Crags

To McCloud

To Highway 89

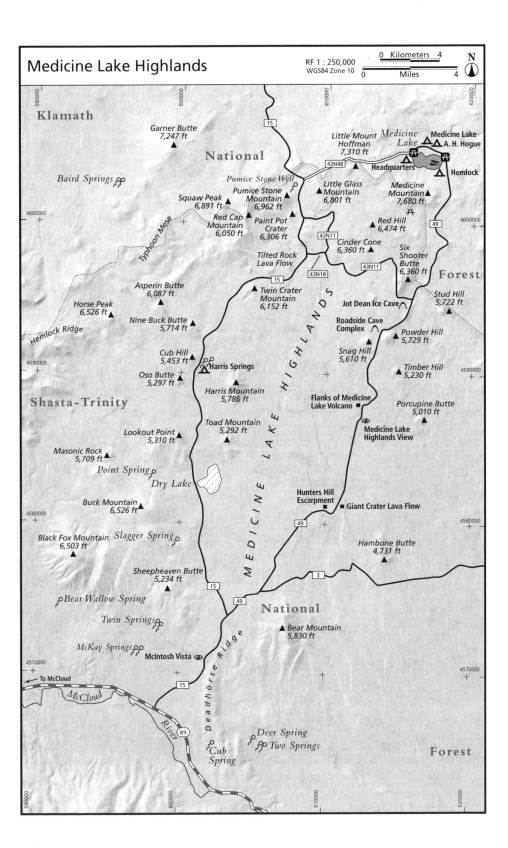

Medicine Lake Highlands

RF 1 : 250,000
WGS84 Zone 10

0 Kilometers 4

0 Miles 4

N

Klamath

Garner Butte
7,247 ft

National

Baird Springs

Pumice Stone Well

Little Mount
Hoffman
7,310 ft

Medicine
Lake

Medicine Lake
A. H. Hogue

43N48

Headquarters

Hemlock

Squaw Peak
6,891 ft

Pumice Stone
Mountain
6,962 ft

Little Glass
Mountain
6,801 ft

Medicine
Mountain
7,680 ft

Red Cap
Mountain
6,050 ft

Paint Pot
Crater
6,306 ft

Red Hill
6,474 ft

Typhoon Mesa

43N11

Cinder Cone
6,360 ft

49

Tilted Rock
Lava Flow

43N18

Six
Shooter
Butte
6,360 ft

43N11

Forest

Asperin Butte
6,087 ft

15

Twin Crater
Mountain
6,152 ft

Jot Dean Ice Cave

Stud Hill
5,722 ft

Horse Peak
6,526 ft

Nine Buck Butte
5,714 ft

Roadside Cave
Complex

Powder Hill
5,729 ft

Hemlock Ridge

Cub Hill
5,453 ft

Harris Springs

Snag Hill
5,610 ft

Timber Hill
5,230 ft

Oso Butte
5,297 ft

Harris Mountain
5,786 ft

Flanks of Medicine
Lake Volcano

Porcupine Butte
5,010 ft

Shasta-Trinity

Toad Mountain
5,292 ft

Medicine Lake
Highlands View

Lookout Point
5,310 ft

Masonic Rock
5,709 ft

Point Spring

Dry Lake

Hunters Hill
Escarpment

Giant Crater Lava Flow

Buck Mountain
6,526 ft

49

Black Fox Mountain
6,503 ft

Slagger Spring

Hambone Butte
4,731 ft

Sheepheaven Butte
5,234 ft

15

3

Bear Wallow Spring

49

National

Twin Springs

Bear Mountain
5,830 ft

McKay Springs

McIntosh Vista

Deadhorse Ridge

To McCloud

15

McCloud

Deer Spring
Two Springs

River

89

Cub
Spring

Forest

MEDICINE LAKE HIGHLANDS

Giant Crater Lava Flow, Medicine Lake Highlands.

many outstanding features aside from its wilderness character. These include not only glaciers but also lava flows, hot springs, and waterfalls.

Mount Shasta attracts people from all over who want to climb it, hike on its slopes, or just look at or photograph the mountain. Although the Mount Shasta Wilderness Area does not have an extensive trail network, a few trails climb partway up its flanks and offer great views of the mountain and the surrounding country. An outstanding scenic drive winds up the south slope of the mountain to end at the timberline.

Those who wish to climb Mount Shasta should be aware that hazards exist, mainly from steep snowslopes, glacial crevasses, rockfall, altitude sickness, and rapidly changing weather. The standard Avalanche Gulch route is not technically difficult, but climbers must be prepared. The climbing season on Mount Shasta runs from May through July. Earlier in the year, deep, soft snow makes the climb a winter mountaineering challenge, and in late summer travel is more difficult as snowfields melt and expose the steep, loose cinder slopes. In addition, rockfall hazard greatly increases as the snowfields vanish. People planning to camp overnight or longer within the Mount Shasta Wilderness Area must have a wilderness permit, which is available at ranger stations and trailheads. In addition, climbers on Mount Shasta must have a Summit Pass to climb above 10,000 feet. Fees are charged for these permits, which are available at ranger stations and self-serve stations at the trailheads.

In the shadow of Mount Shasta to the east lies the much less well known Medicine Lake Highlands. This heavily forested volcanic region is the remains of Medicine Lake Volcano, a broad shield volcano similar to the Hawaiian volcanoes. In contrast to the steep slopes of stratovolcanoes such as Mount Shasta, shield volcanoes are built up from many thin lava flows and have very gently sloped sides. As a result of their gentle slope, shield volcanoes often cover very large areas, and in fact Medicine Lake Volcano is larger in mass than Mount Shasta, and covers an area 15 miles from east to west and 25 miles north to south. Because of the heavy forest and gentle slope, visitors to Medicine Lake often don't realize they are driving up the sides of a volcano.

Medicine Lake Volcano apparently first erupted more than a million years ago. About 100,000 years ago, a series of eruptions resulted in the collapse of the summit area to form a large caldera, which is now partly occupied by Medicine Lake. Some of the many volcanic features in the Medicine Lake Highlands include obsidian flows, extensive pumice deposits, cinder cones, and lava tube caves. The self-guided geology tour explores and explains many of these features. Medicine Lake itself, as well as the several campgrounds on the lake, is in the Modoc National Forest.

Another interesting area near Mount Shasta is the McCloud River, which parallels Highway 89 east of the town of McCloud. Portions of the river flow through deep gorges with waterfalls, and some of the tributary creeks are interesting as well.

Visitor Centers and Amenities

Shasta–Trinity National Forest ranger stations are located in the towns of Mount Shasta and McCloud, where you can obtain maps, books, and brochures, get wilderness permits, and get up-to-date information from rangers. Most trailheads have a self-serve permit station and informative signs. McCloud and Mount Shasta have visitor amenities, including stores, restaurants, and lodging.

Campgrounds

Gumboot Campground is southwest of the town of Mount Shasta at the end of Forest Road 26. It has four units, no water, and no fee.

McBride Springs Campground is partway up the Everitt Memorial Highway on the lower south slopes of Mount Shasta. It has nine units.

Panther Meadows Campground is a walk-in campground near the upper end of the Everitt Memorial Highway. It has ten units, no water, and no fee.

Harris Springs Campground is located on Forest Road 15, in the Medicine Lake Highlands northeast of McCloud. It has fifteen units.

A. H. Hogue, Hemlock, Medicine Lake, and **Headquarters Campgrounds** are small campgrounds located on the shores of Medicine Lake, in the Modoc National Forest. These campgrounds can be reached from the Medicine Lake Highlands Geology Tour road.

Ah-Di-Na Campground is south of McCloud on the McCloud River and the Pacific Crest National Scenic Trail. It is reached by taking paved Forest Road 38N11 and gravel Forest Road 38N53 past McCloud Reservoir. The campground has sixteen units.

Fowlers Camp Campground is east of McCloud on the McCloud River, just south of Highway 89. The Lower Falls of the McCloud River are nearby. The campground has thirty-nine units.

Cattle Camp Campground is just east of McCloud on the south side of Highway 89 at the east end of the McCloud River Loop Road (Forest Road 40N44). It has twenty-five units and is wheelchair-accessible.

Scenic Drives

Everitt Memorial Highway starts from the town of Mount Shasta and climbs to timberline on the south slope of Mount Shasta, a 29.4-mile round trip on a good paved road. From downtown Mount Shasta on Mount Shasta Boulevard, turn northeast on East Lake Street. Drive 0.4 mile, and turn left (north) on

North Washington Drive, which becomes Everitt Memorial Highway (County Road A10) as it leaves town. At 4.7 miles, you'll pass McBride Springs Campground, which is on the left. A viewpoint turnoff at 9 miles has a view of the Shasta Valley, Castle Crags, and the Klamath Mountains to the south and west. At 9.8 miles you'll get the first view of Mount Shasta. Another good viewpoint is at Bunny Flat, which is at 11.2 miles. After the road passes Panther Meadows Campground, it winds upward in several switchbacks to end at the timberline. From here you have a view of Mount Shasta's midlevel slopes, including Sargents Ridge and Green Butte. To the south, the view is panoramic.

McCloud River Loop is an 8-mile drive on gravel roads that wind along a section of the McCloud River, providing access to three fine waterfalls, as well as a picnic area and campground. From McCloud, drive 5.5 miles east on Highway 89, then turn right on the signed road to Fowlers Camp Campground (FR 40N44). Drive 0.5 mile, and turn right on the signed road to Lower Falls. Continue 0.7 mile to Lower Falls Picnic Area. After enjoying the falls, retrace your route 0.7 mile to FR 40N44, and turn right. Drive 1.9 miles to the Upper Falls parking lot, on the right. A short walk leads to an overlook, where you can observe the 60-foot falls. To see the Middle Falls, hike downstream along the rim about 0.2 mile. The scenic drive continues west along FR 40N44, which follows the McCloud River another 3.5 miles, before veering north to return to Highway 89.

Medicine Lake Highlands Scenic Drive is a self-guided geology tour loop drive through the volcanic features of the Medicine Lake Volcano. It is all on paved roads except for 7.2 miles of dirt road west of Medicine Lake. This dirt road portion is passable to most cars if driven with care. To reach the start of the scenic drive from the town of Mount Shasta, drive 29.2 miles east on Highway 89, and turn left onto Harris Springs Road (FR 15). This junction is mile 0.0 for the tour, and you will return here at the end.

0.0 Junction of Highway 89 and FR 15.

2.5 **Deadhorse Ridge,** a prominent ridge on the right, is an upthrown block of a thrust fault. Before the faulting action began thousands of years ago, the ridge and the roadside were at the same elevation.

2.9 **McIntosh Vista** is on the left side of the road, with a great view of Mount Shasta on the right and Castle Crags to the left of Shasta. In the foreground is a forest plantation planted in 1969.

4.4 Turn right onto FR 49 to begin the loop portion of the drive.

11.9 **Hunters Hill Escarpment.** After climbing up the left side of Hunter Hill, the road turns right and descends the steep slope on the north side of the hill, which was created by another fault.

12.3 Giant Crater Lava Flow is intermittently visible alongside the road for the next 10 miles. Watch for gnarled ponderosa pine and incense cedar trees growing out of the jagged rocks.

15.1 Medicine Lake Highlands View. Here you can see the remnants of Medicine Lake Volcano to the north.

15.6 From this point northward to Medicine Lake the road climbs the flanks of Medicine Lake Volcano in a steady ascent of approximately 3,300 feet.

20.6 Roadside Cave Complex. Park on the left side of the road at a pull-out. Scattered around the lava flow to the west of the road are several lava tube caves and natural bridges. These were formed when molten lava cooled and formed a crust on the surface, and still-liquid lava flowed out from underneath. Lava tubes caves can be very short or extend for miles. Nearby **Giant Crater Lava Tube** is the longest known lava tube cave in the world, at nearly 18 miles. If you plan to enter any of the lava tube caves, dress warmly and carry at least two working flashlights.

22.8 Jot Dean Ice Cave is a lava tube cave on the left side of the road. There is a signed parking area. Because cold air tends to collect in lava tube caves, ice may persist throughout the year.

31.0 Medicine Lake partially fills the volcano's caldera, which is 4.5 miles by 6.5 miles. Medicine Lake is 152 feet deep. There is a picnic area, boat launch, and four campgrounds at the lake. To continue the tour, follow the road west along the north side of the lake. It becomes a graded dirt road after leaving the lake.

37.6 Little Glass Mountain is named for the obsidian, or black volcanic glass, that makes up a large part of the flow that created the mountain. Be sure to park in the lot here because it is very easy to get stuck in the loose pumice. Native Americans could not use this obsidian to make tools because of intrusions that make it flake unreliably.

38.4 Turn left on paved FR 15, and head south to continue the scenic drive.

38.7 Pumice Stone Well is marked by a parking area on the right. **Pumice Stone Mountain** is visible across the meadow to the southwest. This cinder cone is covered with pumice that fell during the eruption that created Little Glass Mountain. The well itself is a pond in the meadow that is used by wildlife.

39.4 View of **Little Glass Mountain:** This point offers the best vantage.

40.0 Paint Pot Crater is the red-and-black cinder cone to the west of the road.

Lava tube cave, Medicine Lake Highlands.

41.4 Tilted Rock Lava Flow is 0.7 mile west of the road. The surface of the lava flow cooled before the interior, and the resulting crust broke into tilted pieces as the flow continued to move. High iron content in the lava causes the red color.

45.0 Doe Peak and **Twin Crater Mountain** are to the left, or southeast, of the road. During later periods of eruption, the volcanic vent migrated southward, creating two cones next to each other.

50.1 Harris Springs Campground is 0.75 mile down the short spur road to the left. There is a ranger station here that is open in the summer.

55.4 Dry Lake is east of the paved road and accessible via a short dirt road. This lake was formed during the last glacial period, from 10,000 to 100,000 years ago. It has some water nearly every year, and in wet years it has water year-round. You can see water marks about 4 feet up the trees surrounding the lake.

62.5 FR 49 comes on the left; stay on FR 15 to return to Highway 89.

66.9 Highway 89 and the end of the scenic drive.

Fishing

The upper McCloud River, from Fowlers Camp Campground to McCloud Reservoir, has excellent fishing and is regularly stocked with rainbow trout by the California Department of Fish and Game. Brown trout are also present.

The lower McCloud River, from McCloud Reservoir downstream to Shasta Lake, is a designated Wild Trout Stream and is not stocked. Special fishing regulations apply: Only artificial flies and single barbless hooks can be used. At the McCloud River Preserve, 1 mile downstream from Ah-Di-Na Campground, only catch-and-release fishing is permitted.

In California, the endangered bull trout (also known as Dolly Varden trout) is found only in the McCloud River between Lower Falls and Shasta Lake. It must be released if caught. Check with the California Department of Fish and Game for current regulations. A valid California fishing license is always required.

Finding the Trailheads

On Mount Shasta, the easiest trailheads to reach are the four accessible from the Everitt Memorial Highway on the south slope.

Sand Flat Trailhead provides access to the trail and climbing route up Avalanche Gulch. From downtown Mount Shasta on Mount Shasta Boulevard, turn northeast on East Lake Street. Drive 0.4 mile, and turn left (north) on North Washington Drive, which becomes Everitt Memorial Highway (CR

Along the McCloud River.

A10) as it leaves town. After 9.9 miles, turn left on Sand Flat Road, and continue 1.2 miles to the end of the road.

Bunny Flat Trailhead also provides access to the trail and climbing route up Avalanche Gulch. From downtown Mount Shasta on Mount Shasta Boulevard, turn northeast on East Lake Street. Drive 0.4 mile, and turn left (north) on North Washington Drive, which becomes Everitt Memorial Highway (CR A10) as it leaves town. After 11.2 miles, park in the Bunny Flat lot.

Gray Butte Trailhead provides access to the Gray Butte Trail and is adjacent to Panther Meadows Campground. From downtown Mount Shasta on Mount Shasta Boulevard, turn northeast on East Lake Street. Drive 0.4 mile, and turn left (north) on North Washington Drive, which becomes Everitt Memorial Highway (CR A10) as it leaves town. After 13 miles, park in the Gray Butte lot.

Ski Bowl Trailhead provides access to the Green Butte and Gray Butte Trails. From downtown Mount Shasta on Mount Shasta Boulevard, turn northeast on East Lake Street. Drive 0.4 mile, and turn left (north) on North Washington Drive, which becomes Everitt Memorial Highway (CR A10) as it leaves town. After 13.5 miles, park at the end of the road.

The following two trailheads on the east slope of Mount Shasta are reached by driving long dirt roads through logging areas. Because these roads are constantly changing, plan to follow the Forest Service signs to the trailheads.

Clear Creek Trailhead provides access to the Clear Creek Trail on the southeast slope of Mount Shasta. From the junction of Interstate 5 and Highway 89 just south of the town of Mount Shasta, drive 13 miles east on Highway 89, then turn left on Forest Road 13. This junction is signed for the Mount Shasta Wilderness trailheads. Drive 5.4 miles north and northeast on FR 13, then turn left onto a dirt road signed for Clear Creek Trailhead. Follow the signs to the trailhead.

Brewer Creek Trailhead provides access to the Brewer Creek Trail on the northeast slope of Mount Shasta. From the junction of I–5 and Highway 89 just south of the town of Mount Shasta, drive 13 miles east on Highway 89, then turn left on FR 13. This junction is signed for the Mount Shasta Wilderness trailheads. Drive 7.5 miles north and northeast on FR 13, and turn left onto FR 19, which is a dirt road signed for Brewer Creek Trailhead. Follow the signs to the trailhead.

The final two Mount Shasta trailheads are on the north slope of the mountain and are reached via long dirt roads.

Whitney Falls Trailhead provides access to the Whitney Falls Trail. From the town of Mount Shasta, drive 8.8 miles north on I–5 and exit at Weed. Drive 12.2 miles northeast on U.S. Highway 97, and turn right on Forest Road 43N21. Drive 4 miles south to the end of the road.

North Gate Trailhead provides access to the North Gate Trail. From the town of Mount Shasta, drive 8.8 miles north on I–5 and exit at Weed. Drive 15.1 miles northeast on U.S. 97, and then turn right on Forest Road 43N19, Military Pass Road. Drive 4.7 miles southeast on this dirt road, and turn right on Forest Road 42N16. Drive 3.3 miles, and turn right on Forest Road 42N97A. Drive 0.5 mile to the trailhead.

Cabin Creek Trailhead provides access to the Squaw Valley Creek Trail and Pacific Crest National Scenic Trail. From McCloud on Highway 89, drive 6.2 miles south on Forest Road 11, and turn right on Forest Road 39N21. Continue 3.2 miles to the trailhead.

Lower Falls Trailhead provides access to the McCloud River Trail. There is a picnic area at the trailhead, and Fowlers Camp Campground is nearby. From McCloud, drive 5.5 miles east on Highway 89, and turn right on the signed road to Fowlers Camp Campground (FR 40N44). Drive 0.5 mile, then turn right on the signed road to Lower Falls. Continue 0.7 mile to Lower Falls Picnic Area and park.

Trails

Black Butte

HIGHLIGHTS: A scenic trail to the top of a large cinder cone, offering excellent views of Mount Shasta.

TYPE OF TRIP: Out-and-back.

DISTANCE: 5 miles.

DIFFICULTY: Moderate.

PERMITTED USES: Hiking, horses, mountain biking.

MAPS: Mount Shasta Wilderness (USFS), City of Mount Shasta (USGS).

SPECIAL CONSIDERATIONS: None.

PARKING AND FACILITIES: Trailhead parking is extremely limited; there are a few more parking spots 0.2 mile back down the road.

FINDING THE TRAILHEAD: From downtown Mount Shasta on Mount Shasta Boulevard, turn northeast on East Lake Street. Drive 0.4 mile, and turn left (north) on North Washington Drive, which becomes Everitt Memorial Highway (County Road A10) as it leaves town. After 2.3 miles, just before a sharp right curve, turn left onto Forest Road 41N18 at the sign for Black Butte. Drive 0.1 mile, and turn right to stay on FR 41N18. Drive 1 mile, and turn left to remain on FR 41N18. Continue 0.5 mile, and turn left to stay on FR 41N18. After 0.8 mile, turn left to stay on FR 41N18. Drive 0.3 mile, then turn left

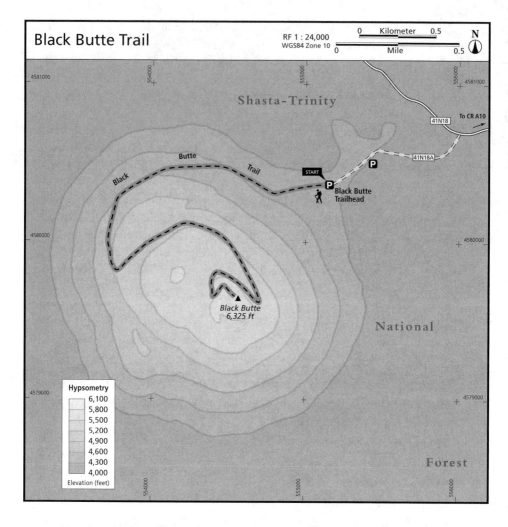

Black Butte Trail

RF 1 : 24,000
WGS84 Zone 10

Shasta-Trinity

To CR A10

41N18

41N18A

Butte

Trail

Black

START

Black Butte
Trailhead

National

Black Butte
6,325 ft

Hypsometry

6,100
5,800
5,500
5,200
4,900
4,600
4,300
4,000
Elevation (feet)

Forest

on Forest Road 41N18A. Drive 0.6 mile to the end of the road on the
northeast slope of Black Butte.

Initially, the Black Butte Trail heads west as it climbs across the lower slopes of
the butte. On the west side, the trail switches back to the east; just below the
summit, it turns west for the final climb to the top. The 6,325-foot summit of
this prominent landmark provides a sweeping view of the Shasta Valley and
Mount Shasta.

KEY POINTS

0.0 Black Butte Trailhead.

2.5 Black Butte.

Black Butte.

Avalanche Gulch

HIGHLIGHTS: An easy and popular hike to Horse Camp, a cabin operated by the Sierra Club.

TYPE OF TRIP: Out-and-back.

DISTANCE: 3.2 miles.

DIFFICULTY: Easy.

PERMITTED USES: Hiking.

MAPS: Mount Shasta Wilderness (USFS), McCloud (USGS).

SPECIAL CONSIDERATIONS: Hikers planning to camp overnight or longer within Mount Shasta Wilderness Area must have a wilderness permit, and climbers ascending above 10,000 feet must have a climbing permit. Permits are available at the trailhead.

PARKING AND FACILITIES: Paved parking area with restrooms.

FINDING THE TRAILHEAD: From downtown Mount Shasta on Mount Shasta Boulevard, turn northeast on East Lake Street. Drive 0.4 mile, and turn left (north) on North Washington Drive, which becomes Everitt Memorial Highway (County Road A10) as it leaves town. After 11.2 miles, park in the Bunny Flat lot.

Starting right from Bunny Flat Trailhead, you have an excellent view of Mount Shasta. The Avalanche Gulch Trail climbs gradually, heading north across a meadow (please stay on the trail, as the vegetation is fragile), then turns northwest through a series of small meadows and isolated stands of the timberline trees. After the Sand Flat Trail comes in from the left, the Avalanche Gulch Trail swings to the northeast and heads directly up the slope. Horse Camp, the goal for this hike, is located right at the timberline in a spectacular setting.

Avalanche Gulch is the starting point for the most popular climbing route to the summit of Mount Shasta.

KEY POINTS

0.0 Bunny Flat Trailhead.

1.0 Sand Flat Trail; turn right to stay on Avalanche Gulch Trail.

1.6 Horse Camp.

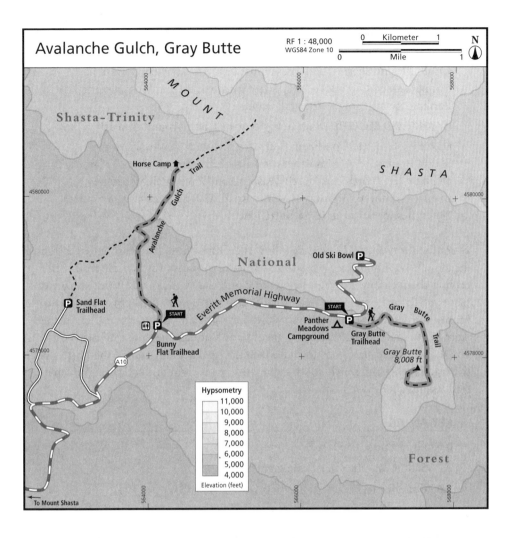

Avalanche Gulch, Gray Butte

Gray Butte

See map above.

HIGHLIGHTS: An easy hike to the summit of a satellite butte on the south slopes of Mount Shasta.

TYPE OF TRIP: Out-and-back.

DISTANCE: 3 miles.

DIFFICULTY: Easy.

PERMITTED USES: Hiking.

MAPS: Mount Shasta Wilderness (USFS), McCloud (USGS).

SPECIAL CONSIDERATIONS: Hikers planning to camp overnight or longer within Mount Shasta Wilderness must have a wilderness permit, and climbers ascending above 10,000 feet must have a climbing permit. Permits are available at the trailhead.

PARKING AND FACILITIES: Panther Meadows Campground is nearby.

FINDING THE TRAILHEAD: From downtown Mount Shasta on Mount Shasta Boulevard, turn northeast on East Lake Street. Drive 0.4 mile, and turn left (north) on North Washington Drive, which becomes Everitt Memorial Highway (County Road A10) as it leaves town. After 13.0 miles, park in the Gray Butte lot.

From the Gray Butte Trailhead, follow the Gray Butte Trail east across a lush meadow. The timberline vegetation is fragile, so please stay on the trail. After leaving the meadow, the trail begins to climb the south slope of the unnamed butte north of Gray Butte, eventually reaching the saddle between the two. Ignore the unofficial trail that branches left, and stay right as the Gray Butte Trail heads south along the east slope of Gray Butte. When the trail turns west, you'll spot a road that goes to radio facilities at the south end of the butte. As the trail reaches the north-south ridge crest, turn right and follow an informal trail to the 8,008-foot summit.

KEY POINTS

0.0 Gray Butte Trailhead.

0.7 Saddle and unofficial trail; stay right.

1.5 Gray Butte.

Clear Creek Springs

HIGHLIGHTS: A timberline hike up the southeast slopes of Mount Shasta to the source of Clear Creek.

TYPE OF TRIP: Out-and-back.

DISTANCE: 4.8 miles.

DIFFICULTY: Moderate.

PERMITTED USES: Hiking.

MAPS: Mount Shasta Wilderness (USFS), McCloud (USGS), Mount Shasta (USGS).

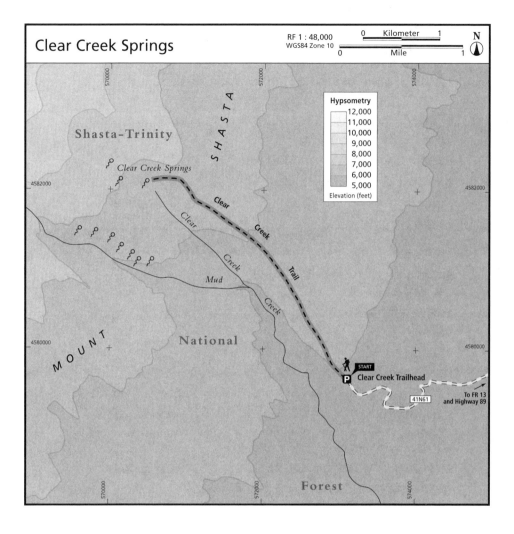

Clear Creek Springs

RF 1 : 48,000
WGS84 Zone 10

Hypsometry
12,000
11,000
10,000
9,000
8,000
7,000
6,000
5,000
Elevation (feet)

Shasta-Trinity

SHASTA

Clear Creek Springs

Clear Creek Trail

Clear

Creek

Mud

Creek

MOUNT

National

Forest

START
Clear Creek Trailhead
P
41N61
To FR 13
and Highway 89

SPECIAL CONSIDERATIONS: Hikers planning to camp overnight or longer within Mount Shasta Wilderness Area must have a wilderness permit, and climbers ascending above 10,000 feet must have a climbing permit. Permits are available at the trailhead.

PARKING AND FACILITIES: Dirt parking area.

FINDING THE TRAILHEAD: From the junction of Interstate 5 and Highway 89 just south of the town of Mount Shasta, drive 13 miles east on Highway 89, and turn left on Forest Road 13. This junction is signed for the Mount Shasta Wilderness trailheads. Drive 5.4 miles north and northeast on FR 13, then turn left onto a dirt road signed for Clear Creek Trailhead. Follow the signs to the trailhead.

From the trailhead, the Clear Creek Trail heads directly northwest up the ridge north of Clear Creek. Shortly after the trail reaches the timberline, you reach the same elevation as the series of springs that are the source for Clear Creek, and an easy traverse to the west leads you to the spring.

KEY POINTS

0.0 Clear Creek Trailhead.

2.1 Traverse west to Clear Creek Springs.

2.4 Clear Creek Springs.

McCloud River Trail

HIGHLIGHTS: This easy trail follows the McCloud River past three spectacular waterfalls.

TYPE OF TRIP: Out-and-back.

DISTANCE: 2.8 miles.

DIFFICULTY: Easy.

PERMITTED USES: Hiking.

MAPS: Shasta–Trinity National Forest (USFS), Lake McCloud (USGS).

SPECIAL CONSIDERATIONS: Use care near rims and overlooks, and on streamside ledges and rocks. When swimming or diving, watch for submerged rocks and obstacles.

PARKING AND FACILITIES: Lower Falls Picnic Area has restrooms.

FINDING THE TRAILHEAD: From McCloud, drive 5.5 miles east on Highway 89, and turn right on the signed road to Fowlers Camp Campground (Forest Road 40N44). Drive 0.5 mile, then turn right on the signed road to Lower Falls. Continue 0.7 mile to Lower Falls Picnic Area, and park.

Lower Falls is next to the picnic area; follow the trail along the west bank of the McCloud River. Here the McCloud River plunges over a basalt ledge for about 15 feet, forming a barrier to the upstream migration of salmon. Follow the trail along the west and north side of the river past the edge of Fowlers Camp Campground. A roar announces Middle Falls, where the river plunges about 30 feet. Follow the trail up to the rim north of the river. An easy walk leads to the overlook above Upper Falls, which is by far the highest of the three falls, at about 60 feet.

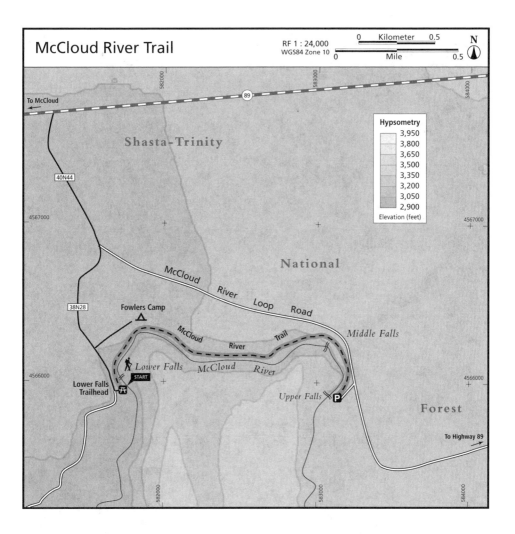

KEY POINTS

0.0 Lower Falls Trailhead.

1.0 Middle Falls.

1.4 Upper Falls.

Upper Falls, McCloud River Trail.

Appendix
For More Information

Bureau of Land Management
Redding Field Office
355 Hemsted Drive
Redding, CA 96002
(530) 224–2100
www.ca.blm.gov/redding

Castle Crags State Park
Castella, CA 96017
(530) 235–2684 or
(530) 225–2065
www.parks.ca.gov/

Modoc National Forest
800 West Twelfth Street
Alturas, CA 96101
(530) 233–5811
www.fs.fed.us/r5/modoc

Shasta Lake Ranger Station and
  Visitor Center
14250 Holiday Road
Redding, CA 96003
(530) 275–1589
www.fs.fed.us/r5/shastatrinity/
  recreation/nra/visitor-center.shtml

Shasta–Trinity National Forest
Big Bar Ranger Station
Star Route 1, Box 10
(28451 State Highway 299 West)
Big Bar, CA 96010
(530) 623–6106
www.fs.fed.us/r5/shastatrinity

Shasta–Trinity National Forest
McCloud Ranger Station
P.O. Box 1620
2019 Forest Road
McCloud, CA 96057
(530) 964–2184
www.fs.fed.us/r5/shastatrinity

Shasta–Trinity National Forest
Mount Shasta Ranger Station
204 West Alma Street
Mount Shasta, CA 96067
(530) 926–4511
www.fs.fed.us/r5/shastatrinity

Shasta–Trinity National Forest
Weaverville Ranger Station
P.O. Box 1190
210 Main Street
Weaverville, CA 96093
(530) 623–2121
www.fs.fed.us/r5/shastatrinity

Whiskeytown National Recreation
  Area
P.O. Box 188
Whiskeytown, CA 96095
(530) 242–3400
www.nps.gov/whis

Index

W

waste disposal, 7
water access, Trinity River, 50–51
water purification, 15
waterskiing
   rules, 9
   Shasta Lake Unit, 100
   Whiskeytown Lake Unit, 34
Weather, 12–13
Weaverville, 45, 48, 53, 55, 58, 78
Whiskey Creek, 33–34
Whiskeytown Cemetery, 35

Whiskeytown Dam, 34
Whiskeytown Lake, 31, 34, 53
Whiskeytown Lake Unit:
   Whiskeytown–Shasta–Trinity
   National Recreation Area, 21,
   31–43
whitewater rafting, 45, 50–51
windsurfing, 34

Z

Zero impact, 5–8

About the Author

Bruce Grubbs is an avid hiker, mountain biker, paddler, and cross-country skier who has been exploring the American West for more than thirty-five years. An active outdoor writer and photographer, he's written eighteen outdoor guidebooks, and his photos have been published in *Backpacker* and other magazines. He is also an active charter pilot and lives in Flagstaff, Arizona. His other FalconGuides include:

Hiking Arizona

Hiking Northern Arizona

Best Easy Day Hikes Flagstaff

Best Easy Day Hikes Sedona

Camping Arizona

Hiking Arizona's Superstition and Mazatzal County

Mountain Biking Phoenix

Mountain Biking Flagstaff and Sedona

Basic Essentials: Using GPS

Desert Hiking Tips

Hiking Nevada

Hiking Great Basin National Park

Hiking Oregon's Central Cascades

Mountain Biking St. George and Cedar City

A FalconGuide to Saguaro National Park and the Santa Catalina Mountains

For more information, check the author's Web site at www.brucegrubbs.com.